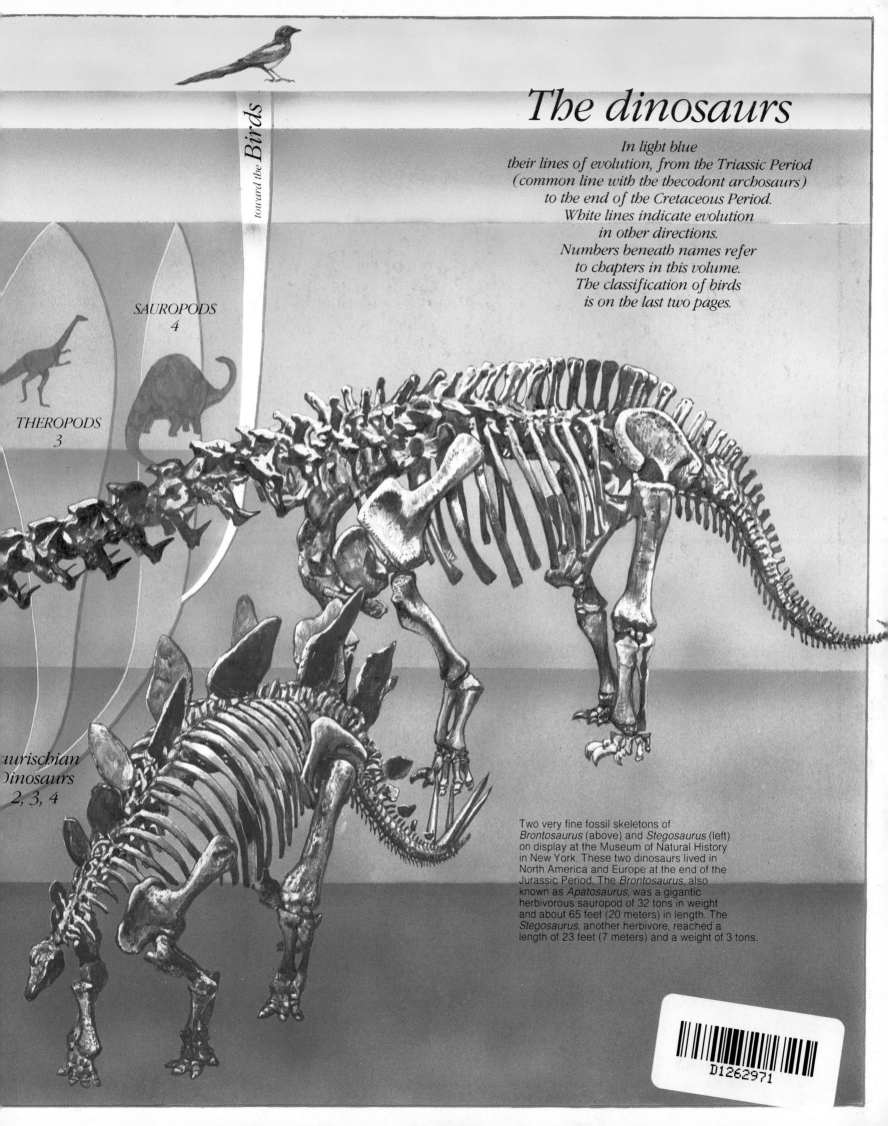

The dinosaurs

*In light blue
their lines of evolution, from the Triassic Period
(common line with the thecodont archosaurs)
to the end of the Cretaceous Period.
White lines indicate evolution
in other directions.
Numbers beneath names refer
to chapters in this volume.
The classification of birds
is on the last two pages.*

toward the Birds

SAUROPODS
4

THEROPODS
3

aurischian
Dinosaurs
2, 3, 4

Two very fine fossil skeletons of
Brontosaurus (above) and *Stegosaurus* (left)
on display at the Museum of Natural History
in New York. These two dinosaurs lived in
North America and Europe at the end of the
Jurassic Period. The *Brontosaurus*, also
known as *Apatosaurus*, was a gigantic
herbivorous sauropod of 32 tons in weight
and about 65 feet (20 meters) in length. The
Stegosaurus, another herbivore, reached a
length of 23 feet (7 meters) and a weight of 3 tons.

THE HISTORY OF LIFE ON EARTH

DINOSAURS AND BIRDS

© 1987 English-language edition by Facts On File, Inc.
460 Park Avenue South, New York, NY 10016

© 1987 Editoriale Jaca Book Spa, Milano

editorial coordination

CATERINA LONGANESI

CONTENTS

1. The Dinosaurs in History
2. The Ramifications
3. Saurischian Dinosaurs (*Theropods*)
4. Saurischian Dinosaurs (*Sauropods*)
5. Ornithischian Dinosaurs (*Ornithopods* and *Ankylosaurs*)
6. The Other Ornithischians (*Stegosaurs* and *Ceratopsians*)
7. The Pterosaurs
8. The Death of the Dinosaurs: Biological Causes
9. The Death of the Dinosaurs: Astronomical Causes
10. Origin of Birds
11. Extinct Birds
12. Modern Birds
13. How They Breathe and How They Eat
14. The Skeleton
15. Flight
16. Intelligence
17. Color
18. Nest, Eggs, Parental Care
19. Migrations
20. Extinct Running Birds
21. Living Running Birds
22. Penguins and Auks
23. Vultures, Eagles, and Falcons
24. Nocturnal Birds of Prey
25. Hummingbirds and Quetzals
26. Toucans, Woodpeckers, Parrots
27. Marsh Birds
28. The Passeriformes

Library of Congress Cataloging-in-Pubblication Data

Minelli, G.
  Dinosaurs and birds.

  (History of life on earth)
  Translation of: Dinosauri e uccelli.
  Summary: Discusses evolution theories relating dinosaurs and birds.
  1. Evolution—Juvenile literature. 2. Vertebrates—Evolution—Juvenile literature. 3. Paleontology—Juvenile literature. [1. Evolution. 2. Dinosaurs] I. Orlandi, Lorenzo, ill. II. Title. III. Series.
  QH367.1.M5613 1988 567.9'1 87-9180
  ISBN 0-8160-1559-7

color separation by
Carlo Scotti, Milan
photosetting by
Elle Due, Milan
printed and bound in Italy by
Tipolitografia G. Canale & C. Spa, Turin

DINOSAURS AND BIRDS

Giuseppe Minelli

professor of Comparative Anatomy
University of Bologna, Italy

illustrated by the

Lorenzo Orlandi Studio

translated by

Margaret Meringer

the "History of Life on Earth" series
is conceived, designed and produced by

Jaca Book

Facts On File Publications
New York, New York ● Oxford, England

As time passes, other layers are formed and the process of mineralization begins in the skeleton. Bones have large numbers of small holes, or pores, that are filled by minerals in the ground. In this way they are petrified, turning into rock inside rock.

Ceratosaurus

In 1884 the remains of the *Ceratosaurus*, a carnivorous dinosaur from the Jurassic Period, about 20 feet (6 meters) long, were found in Colorado by Marsh. Fossilization of this reptile, like that of any animal, took place gradually. On the animal's death the soft parts of its body decompose, while the bones are covered by layers of mud.

1. THE DINOSAURS IN HISTORY

Only 150-200 years ago nothing was known of a spectacular and long-lasting period of time millions of years earlier: the presence of life forms on our planet that were completely different from those we see today. It was not known that for over 100 million years all corners of the Earth had been occupied by dinosaur reptiles. When some parts of their skeletons by chance came to light, it was looked upon as a "freak of nature," especially since fossilization causes bones to take on the appearance of stones. Every now and then, some more attentive observer put forward different suggestions, but skepticism was general. At the beginning of the last century, with the French scholar Georges Cuvier (1769-1832), paleontology—the science that studies the oldest forms of life on the basis of fossil discoveries—was born, and the figure of one of the most extraordinary protagonists in the history of vertebrates, the dinosaur, or "terrible lizard" according to the meaning of the Greek word from which the term derives, began to take shape before the researchers' eyes.

In 1795, the French revolutionary army besieged a fortress near Maastricht, a town in Holland. Once the resistance of the defenders was overcome, the troops were ordered to search the fort to take possession of a primitive relic, which was famous in the civilized world. The relic consisted of the skull and two jaw-bones of a gigantic creature discovered in a chalk quarry. However, the victorious troops arrived too late; the owner of the precious skull had already removed it. This is perhaps the first historic event connected with the discovery of reptile fossils, and bears witness to the great interest aroused by these extinct animals.

THE RUSH TO DISCOVER DINOSAURS

The real "fever of the dinosaur hunt" burst out in the second half of the nineteenth century, when all the natural history museums and the cultural and scientific institutions were anxious to own dinosaur skeletons. Thus, the most varied expeditions were organized in order to identify deposits of fossils. A bitter struggle arose to find the strangest, largest, most terrible dinosaur. In this competition it was above all the Americans Edward Drinker Cope (1840-1897) and Othniel Charles Marsh (1831-1899) who distinguished themselves. Friends at first, but then implacable rivals, they made their searches in the fossil-bearing jurassic and cretaceous layers of the United States. Their emissaries, acting in the utmost secrecy, tirelessly roamed these territories in search of a sign that would give reason to expect the presence of fossils. Any discovery was reported in great secrecy to Cope or Marsh, who would hasten to organize an expedition. To prevent his rival from learning the place of excavation, each explorer would start in the wrong direction and only set out towards the selected spot after zigzagging to put observers off the scent. Excavations were carried out in a frantic rush, all available fossils had to be extracted before the adversary learned of the discovery; then on completion of the work, everything left was destroyed

2

In later periods the earth undergoes various changes and deeper layers may be brought to the surface. Wind and rain then erode the rock, revealing the presence of fossils.

When paleontologists discover a fossil they excavate right round it, trying to remove it as intact as possible, so as to be able to reconstruct it in the museum.

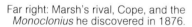

Far right: Marsh's rival, Cope, and the *Monoclonius* he discovered in 1876.

A souvenir photograph of Marsh (standing) and two of his pupils.

Monoclonius

...ith dynamite charges in the fear that the rival might ...sume the search in the same locality. This crazy ...ompetition at least resulted in discovery of ...umerous species of dinosaurs within a few decades, ...en carefully reconstructed in the laboratories.

RESEARCH TODAY

...hen the exploits of Cope and Marsh came to an end, ...ricter investigations were started, not so much with ...e aim of discovering sensational specimens as to ...prove general knowledge about this exceptional ...oup of vertebrates. Today, it is relatively unimportant ... discover a new species of dinosaur; it is of greater ...terest to locate traces that will give us information ... how these creatures lived, what they fed on, what ...eir metabolism was like, and what diseases they ...ffered from. To do this it is not enough to collect ...ssil bones on the spot. When a fossil rock has been ...scovered, it is taken as a block to a laboratory, where ...e different bones can be extracted calmly, along ...th a detailed study of everything that surrounds the ...scovery.

FOSSILIZATION

The chances of an animal's carcass being preserved through time are low. In order to fossilize, the skeleton must quickly be removed from the chemical attacks of the environment. Rain, for example, tends to extract the mineral component from bones, while microorganisms destroy the organic part. A sandstorm may bury the carcass or the flooding of a river may drag it into the river delta where it will be covered by sediment; a pool of viscid bitumen or treacherous clay may entrap an unfortunate animal forever. Once

the skeleton has been covered, the sediment is eventually converted to rock, incorporating the bones which are in turn infiltrated by mineral crystals. The chances of a skeleton being fossilized also depend on the anatomical characteristics of the animal, and on the environment in which it has lived. For example, we know very little about the theriodont therapsids, mammal-like reptiles, because they were generally very small animals, no larger than a rat, and lived in the dark undergrowth of the forests where a swarm of other living creatures quickly destroyed their carcasses.

Fossil footprints of *Chiroterium*.

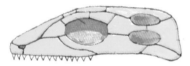

The dinosaurs are diapsid reptiles, i.e. with two openings (pink) in the side wall of the skull.

The *Ornithosuchus*, one of the most primitive dinosaurs, was carnivorous and bipedal, and had a long tail to balance its body weight when running. About 3 feet (1 meter) long, it lived in the Triassic Period.

Ornithosuchus

2. THE RAMIFICATIONS

THE EVOLUTIONARY LINE TO THE ORIGIN OF THE DINOSAURS

In the volume *Reptiles* we saw the different evolutionary lines of the great class of reptiles. Among these, in the Triassic Period, the thecodont archosaurs emerged; these had two lateral openings on the skull (diapsids) and teeth firmly embedded into the jaw sockets, a characteristic which in fact gives them the Greek name "thecodonts." They were the ancestors of the dinosaurs. The thecodont archosaurs were, however, the matrix of other evolutionary lines of the reptiles, including the loricates, which have come down to us with the crocodiles, and the now extinct pterosaurs, the first vertebrates capable of flying.

THE FOOTPRINTS OF THE *CHIROTHERIUM*

The first certain tracks of dinosaurs date from the Triassic Period, over 200 million years ago. Almost everywhere, especially in Europe, North and South America, and South Africa, mysterious fossil footprints were found and aroused long years of discussion

before they were identified. Discovered in 1824, they were first attributed to a man or a large ape, called *Paleopithecus*, then to a big toad, then to a reptile, and finally to a mammal to which the name of *Chirotherium* was given. In 1925, the discussions came to an end; the footprints were those of a dinosaur, as was demonstrated by the fact that the forelimbs were much smaller and weaker than the hind ones. The dinosaurs were the first vertebrates to assume an erect position, and to move more quickly than their four-footed reptiles contemporaries. Perhaps this development was their winning card: with speed it is easier to prey, and it is also possible to flee more rapidly from other marauders.

DEVELOPMENT OF THE DINOSAURS

In the Triassic Period 80% of the reptiles were therapsids, an evolutionary line different from that of the dinosaurs (see *Reptiles*, Chap. 13). The competition between the two lines was at once settled in favor of the dinosaurs, which established themselves throughout the Earth, at that time joined

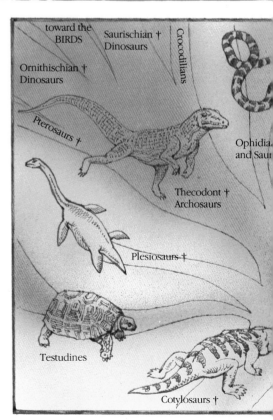

toward the BIRDS
Saurischian †
Dinosaurs
Crocodilians
Ornithischian †
Dinosaurs
Pterosaurs †
Ophidia and Saur
Thecodont † Archosaurs
Plesiosaurs †
Testudines
Cotylosaurs †

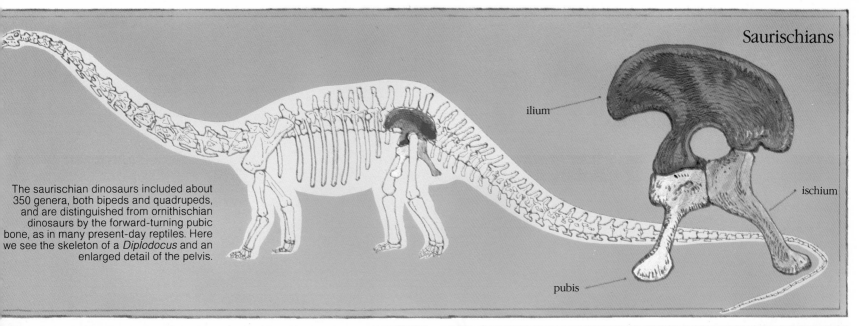

The saurischian dinosaurs included about 350 genera, both bipeds and quadrupeds, and are distinguished from ornithischian dinosaurs by the forward-turning pubic bone, as in many present-day reptiles. Here we see the skeleton of a *Diplodocus* and an enlarged detail of the pelvis.

ilium

ischium

pubis

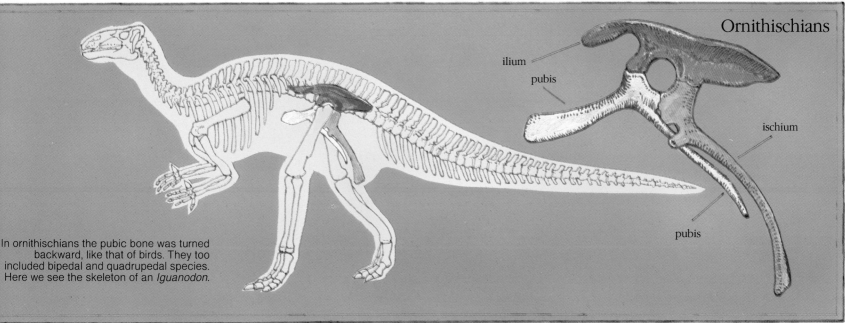

Ornithischians

ilium

pubis

ischium

pubis

In ornithischians the pubic bone was turned backward, like that of birds. They too included bipedal and quadrupedal species. Here we see the skeleton of an *Iguanodon*.

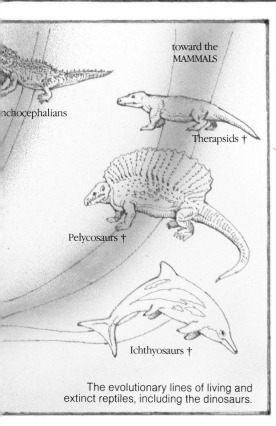

toward the MAMMALS

nchocephalians

Therapsids †

Pelycosaurs †

Ichthyosaurs †

The evolutionary lines of living and extinct reptiles, including the dinosaurs.

into a single supercontinent, Pangaea. The therapsids disappeared and the reign of the dinosaurs lasted for an incredibly long time, about 120 million years, down to the end of the Cretaceous Period. It is strange, however, that apparently no dinosaur ventured into the open waters: the many reptiles that adapted themselves to marine life during this period belonged to very different evolutionary lines from that of the dinosaurs.

THE SAURISCHIANS

Among the dinosaurs, two directions of evolution can be observed, based on the characteristics of the pelvis. In the saurischians the arrangement of the pelvic bones was typical of reptiles, with the sole difference that the ilium was very large and was articulated with numerous vertebrae of the spinal column while the pubic bone was directed forward. In four-footed reptiles the ilium is articulated only with two vertebrae in the sacral region of the spinal column, and the weight of the body is distributed equally on the four limbs. But in the dinosaurs, which originally raised themselves on their hind paws in order to assume a biped gait, the entire body-weight was supported on the pelvis and hind limbs, giving rise to

the need for a more ample ratio between ilium and the sacral region of the spinal column. The saurischian dinosaurs included huge biped carnivores such as *Tyrannosaurus rex*, often depicted in drawings and animated cartoons, and colossal herbivores that had returned to walking on four legs and which probably led an amphibian life in order to discharge part of their weight, of 20-50 tons, onto the water. Not all the saurischians were gigantic; there were also very minute and elegant forms: from these a new class, that of the birds, perhaps took its origin.

THE ORNITHISCHIANS

The other evolutionary line of dinosaurs, the ornithischians, had a pelvis similar to that of present-day birds, with the pubic bone directed backward. The ornithischians also had a very large ilium, and, consequently, ample articulation between pelvis and spinal column. They were herbivorous and included stegosaurs, with their backs bristling with large bony plates; horned ceratopsians; ankylosaurs, with their body almost entirely covered with a bony armor for defense; and ornithopods—among which we shall see the "duck-billed dinosaurs" and the *Iguanodon*—huge in stature, biped and amphibian.

Compsognathus

A comparison between the skeletons of three vertebrates with a bipedal gait. In the *Tyrannosaurus* and kangaroo the weight of the forward-leaning body is balanced by the heavy tail.

Tyrannosaurus

Kangaroo

Man

About 25 inches (65 centimeters) long, the *Compsognathus* was one of the smallest dinosaurs. It lived around the tropical lagoons that covered much of what is now France and Germany during the Jurassic Period. Carnivorous but small, its prey must have been other small reptiles and insects like dragonflies. The birds may have evolved out of this animal.

3. SAURISCHIAN DINOSAURS
(Theropods)

The branch of saurischians is separated into two large groups, the theropods with a strictly carnivorous diet, and the herbivorous sauropods (which we shall look at in the next chapter).

THE TAIL AND PAWS OF THEROPODS

Theropod dinosaurs may have spectacular forms which excite visitors to museums housing their skeletons, or minute and not very striking forms which are nonetheless of great scientific interest. Whether large or small, they all have erect posture—or, in other words, they are bipeds—and therefore the weight of the body, in order not to fall forward, is balanced by the large and heavy tail. The hind paws are powerful and very well developed, while the forepaws are small, and in the really gigantic theropods seem to be useless stumps. It was thought, at first, that they had atrophied and were no longer of any use, but then it was discovered that with these small limbs, which were provided with claws, the animal could stop the prey it was hunting or obtain help in a difficult operation. Even dinosaurs lay down on the ground to rest, but it must have been a problem to get up again with only the hind paws: grasping

some kind of support with these little hands may have been the solution.

TYRANNOSAURUS REX

With its height of over 16 feet (5 meters), it was the giant of the Earth's carnivores. It had an enormous mouth bristling with sharp teeth, while the powerful lower jaw enabled it to open its mouth wide in order to seize its prey. The animal must have constituted a constant danger for any other living form, especially since it was presumably able to run fairly fast for short distances. The hind limbs are in fact sturdy and, from the footprints left by a running *Tyrannosaurus,* are found to be nearly 13 feet (4 meters) from each other. For rapid running, a high metabolism is also necessary, so it cannot be excluded that these reptiles were capable of maintaining a constant temperature; but we shall examine this question more fully in a later chapter. The *Tyrannosaurus* was not the only giant of its time; other species, such as the *Gorgosaurus,* exhibited the same characteristics. Alongside the carnivores lived real mountains of flesh, the herbivorous dinosaurs, which constituted the carnivores' favorite food and their main source of energy.

From a crouching position (**1**), the *Tyrannosaurus* used its tiny forelegs to give it the thrust (**2**) needed prevent it from falling forward when rising to an upright position (**3**).

THE SMALL THEROPODS

While the public admires the *Tyrannosaurus,* th researcher is fascinated by the study of the mo minute forms of theropods. The *Compsognathus,* f example, little larger than a hen, is the smalle dinosaur that we know. Like all the theropods it w carnivorous, but possessed an agile, elegant body ar a light skeleton. The long paws, well furnished wi muscle, let us suppose it was a good runner. The fan and interest of the *Compsognathus* is also linked the hypothesis that this little dinosaur may have bee

Tyrannosaurus

Trachodon

Provided with about 60 sharp teeth for tearing flesh, this fossil skull of a *Tyrannosaurus*, just over 3 feet (1 meter) long, testifies to the bulk and voracity of this fearsome carnivore from the Cretaceous Period. Upper and lower jaw could be opened very wide, allowing large pieces of flesh to be swallowed.

the origin of the great class of birds. The skeletal resemblances between the *Compsognathus* and the oldest bird are so surprising, some researchers put forward the hypothesis that these dinosaurs were themselves primitive birds. We shall, in fact, see that the most ancient bird, the *Archaeopteryx*, is recognized as a bird and not as a reptile, only because of the impression of feathers around its skeleton— otherwise it has typically reptilian characteristics.

INTELLIGENCE

Now that the frenzied chase after the largest and most spectacular dinosaur is over, attempts are being made, especially in the smaller specimens, to study the development of a characteristic that does not fossilize: intelligence. The problem is highly complex and difficult to resolve; intelligence can certainly not be identified or connected with a smaller or larger brain mass, but there is no doubt that a high intelligence cannot develop from a tiny brain. From this standpoint, the saurischian dinosaurs lie exactly at the two extremes. As we shall see in the next chapter, the herbivorous giants had a very small brain, and hence they must in all probability have been stupid, whereas there are quite a few species of theropods that had a ratio between brain volume and body volume very similar or superior to that of some orders of mammals. Among these reptiles a more evolved and probably more intelligent mode of reacting emerged. Unfortunately, however, these researches are only in the early stages; an attempt is also being made to take casts of the cranial cavity in order to see which parts of the brain were most or least developed.

Fossil remains of the *Tyrannosaurus* have been found in North America. In spite of its awesome appearance, the mouth was used more for tearing up the prey than for attacking it. The reptile used its large hind limbs to strike and immobilize its victims. It is believed to have usually fed on herbivorous dinosaurs, such as this *Trachodon*, very widespread at the time.

4. SAURISCHIAN DINOSAURS
(Sauropods)

The saurischians hold the record size for a land vertebrate; only the great whales can compete with them, even though for the cetaceans the weight problem is resolved by Archimedes' principle: it is the water that holds up the whale's body. The herbivorous giants, on the other hand, discharge their weight onto the land through their limbs, and hence the necessity for monstruously colossal paws.

THE HERBIVOROUS GIANTS

The sauropods derive from the prosauropods, a group of saurischian bipeds that lived in the Triassic Period; these animals were still partially carnivorous, while the sauropods had a strictly herbivorous diet, or nearly so. Unlike the other dinosaurs, these herbivores returned to walking on four paws, but the lesser development of the front limbs reveals their origin from biped forms. The four footed position, herbivorous diet, and wide availability of food quickly led to gigantism. The *Diplodocus* and the *Brontosaurus* weighed tens of tons; the record seems however to belong to the *Brachiosaurus*, which perhaps reached and exceeded 100 tons. A puzzle at once arises however; even though the paws are strong and powerful—some femurs exceeded 6.5 feet (2 meters) in length, with a diameter of more than 20 inches (50 centimeters)—it is not thought that they were capable of supporting a load of 50-60 tons for long. Especially if it is borne in mind that when a quadruped moves its weight rests on only three paws, since one of the four is always in the air, and if it is remembered that the hind paws received the greater load, the hypothesis that these animals led a mainly amphibian life so as to discharge their body weight on sufficiently deep waters must be formed.

WHAT THEY FED ON: GRAZING ON SEAWEED

The second, and no less mysterious, puzzle is the diet of these colossal creatures. First, because in many species the head was incredibly small, it is difficult to see how the dinosaur could swallow the enormous quantity of food required for its immense body. Moreover, if the sauropods led an amphibious life and fed on seaweeds or lacustrian plants, a further complicated problem arises since these plants, even though they are easily digestible, have little nutritive value owing to their high water content. Thus, an even greater quantity of food would have had to pass through this small mouth.

GRAZING ON TREES

The problem is so complex that some researchers have dropped the idea of amphibian sauropods and suggested other hypotheses. For example, it has been surmised that these giants moved out of the water and used their long necks to graze on the tops of trees, where the tender shoots might offer food of higher nutritive value. The hypothesis is interesting, but

A herd of *Brontosaurus* grazing in a North American swamp during the Jurassic Period.

Yellow inset: H.W. Mencke posing alongside an enormous *Brachiosaurus* femur discovered in 1900.

Brontosaurus

Brachiosaurus

According to recent theories by some scientists, the long neck of the *Brachiosaurus*, some 43 feet (13 meters) in height, allowed it to browse tender leaves and shoots from tree tops that were out of reach of other animals, like a colossal giraffe.

unfortunately neglects two difficulties: the first, which we have already considered, is linked to the problem of weight, while the latter concerns the extreme danger for these slow and lazy herbivorous giants living on land in close contact with the terrible carnivores; water must then also have constituted a secure haven for the sauropods.

DENTITION

In the sauropods' mouths one would expect to find dentition adequate for herbivorous feeding, but these mysterious animals present another surprise: they are almost toothless! The few teeth, located at the end of the snout, are small forward-turned cylinders, suitable certainly for tearing off vegetable material, but a little at a time. There have been suggestions of a different diet based on molluscs torn from the sand and crushed with these strange teeth. The hypothesis must be discarded, however, as no large quantities of crushed mollusc shells have ever been found in places inhabited by sauropods. Alongside the skeletons of these animals, on the other hand, round stones called gastrolytes have been found, and these may have come from the stomachs of these dinosaurs. It is, therefore, likely that, like birds, sauropods had stomachs capable of masticating with the help of stones and pebbles.

The head of the *Diplodocus*, tiny in relation to its body, had a mouth crammed with incisors. It is thought to have used these for tearing up grass, or even for crushing the shells of molluscs.

Diplodocus

The *Diplodocus*, which exceeded 85 feet (26 meters) in length, was distinguished from other sauropods by the length and slenderness of its neck and tail.

THE BRAIN

brain
encephalon

cervical
intumescence

lumbar
intumescence

Control of this enormous mass of flesh was entrusted to a most unusual brain, or rather to three brains. In fact, at the junctions of the fore and hind limbs the spinal cord is greatly enlarged, while the true brain is extremely small, enclosed inside the very tiny head. Considering the size of their bodies, the gigantic herbivores should have had a proportionally large head, but the volume of the skull is incredibly small. It is difficult to imagine any ray of intelligence in these animals; perhaps they were enormous and totally stupid machines that continuously converted vegetable matter to flesh. With this structure, the sauropods were extremely fragile and their existence was linked to many favorable circumstances, such as large quantities of food and water; hence, it is not surprising that they disappeared when there was a change in the environment, and with them the great carnivores.

Right: sauropods had very small brains (that of the *Diplodocus* resembled a hen's egg) but this was offset by the fact that they had an extra two, known as intumescences, located close to the fore and hind limbs.

Also known as "duck-billed dinosaurs", these ornithopods were scattered over every continent during the Cretaceous Period. The major finds have been in North and South America, Europe and eastern Asia.

Parasaurolophus

Trachodon

Corythosaurus

Head and lower jaw of *Corythosaurus*.

5. ORNITHISCHIAN DINOSAURS
(Ornithopods and Ankylosaurs)

The second great evolutionary path of the dinosaurs, that of the ornithischians, has some spectacular forms, though not as huge as the saurischians'. The ornithischians, which owe their name to the pelvic bones—similar to those of birds—had biped and quadruped forms, characterized by forelimbs different from hind limbs, giving reason to suppose a biped origin. The diet of the ornithischians was almost exclusively herbivorous, and the dentition very specialized. They are divided into four independent lines of evolution: the ornithopods, ankylosaurs, stegosaurs and ceratopsians.

THE ORNITHOPODS

They were the only ornithischians with erect posture. Their forelimbs were not useless stumps, however, but strong and sometimes armed with a long, sharp thumb. Many were amphibian, and, in fact, mummified ornithopods have been found with a membrane between the toes like that of swimming birds. Their body was very similar to that of the big biped carnivores: the weight thrust forward was compensated by a strong tail. In some cases, the tail was rather stiff and during movement whipped

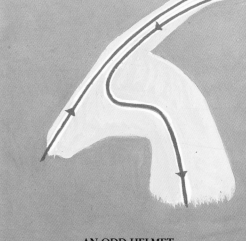

AN ODD HELMET

The skull of the *Parasaurolophus* had a hollow crest up to 6.5 feet (2 meters) long. The arrows indicate the route taken by the air through the crest before entering the lungs.
It probably served as a resonance chamber to improve the animal's hearing.

Early reconstructions depicted the *Iguanodon* as an enormous lizard with a horn on its nose. The correct form illustrated here was not worked out until later. It lived during the Cretaceous Period in Europe, Asia, North Africa and North America.

Iguanodon

Scholosaurus

Ankylosaurus

The *Scholosaurus* and *Ankylosaurus* were widespread in North America during the Cretaceous Period. When attacked they dug into the ground and buried themselves partially, their upper parts protected by a formidable bony armor.

ngerously to the right and left; specimens of these nosaurs suffered fractures of the tail vertebrae that bsequently healed up again. The ornithopods esented decidedly unusual forms: the *Trachodon* easured up to 32 feet (10 meters) in length and had duck-billed mouth armed with about 2,000 teeth lily arranged in parallel rows. The *Kritosaurus* was kewise furnished with this formidable battery of eth, probably specialized for grinding up vegetable atter. Moreover, these dinosaurs had no defenses, either offensive nor defensive, and it must be sumed that they entrusted their safety to a refined vareness of danger, from which they endeavored to cape by throwing themselves into the swamp water.

STRANGE HEADS

he ornithopods of amphibious habits had extremely range heads, like the duck-billed head of the

Trachodon, or the *Corythosaurus* head surmounted by a crest, similar to a helmet, or the *Parasaurolophus'* head, with a hollow tubular extension toward the back through which air was taken in.

IGUANODON

With this ornithopod there is a return to normality: nothing strange or unusual in its skeleton, except that the thumbs of its forelimbs were converted to a sharp dagger. The *Iguanodon* must have been very common in Europe; in Belgium, a sediment has been discovered that contains no fewer than 23 complete or almost complete skeletons: a real cemetery! The *Iguanodon* had the traditional form of the biped dinosaur, and was a very respectable size, up to 16 feet (5 meters) tall and nearly 32 feet (10 meters) long. Its diet was herbivorous, the teeth serrated and suitable for grinding up vegetable matter.

THE ANKYLOSAURS

This suborder of ornithischians includes those forms that entrusted the problem of survival to the heavy bony armor on the head and the entire body. The ankylosaurs returned to movement on four paws, thus renouncing the advantages of speed. The dinosaur, in view of the weight of its body, was obliged to move slowly, contenting itself with proceeding from one place to another in search of new pastures. The *Scholosaurus,* for example, more than 16 feet (5 meters) long, had heavy bony plates on its back, arranged in order and provided with conical protuberances. The strong tail, furnished with two sharp projections, constituted an important means of defense—indeed the only one the *Scholosaurus* had. Perhaps the only way to catch ankylosaurs was to turn them onto their backs, thus exposing the defenseless underbelly.

11

Stegosaurus

Tyrannosaurus

The first *Stegosaurus* was discovered by Marsh in Colorado in 1877. Since then other fossil remains dating from the Jurassic Period have been found in other areas of North America and in England.

6. THE OTHER ORNITHISCHIANS

(Stegosaurs and Ceratopsians)

THE STEGOSAURS

This suborder includes the ornithischian dinosaurs furnished with enormous bony plates on the back. These reptiles, mainly found in North America, reached a length of 29.5 feet (9 meters) from the small head to the tip of the tail. The body was massive, with an arched spinal column, so that head and tail were at ground level. The heavy, stocky limbs prevented fast movement. The animal's defense was entrusted to the sturdy tail, ending with four long, sharp projections. Lashes from this tail must have been particularly dangerous for the aggressor and caused deep wounds.

THE BACK PLATES

But the most typical characteristic of the stegosaurs lies in the two series of bony plates arranged on the back, running from the neck to the tail. It was thought that, together with the lashing tail, these plates were a weapon of defense against the bites of carnivores. It has, however, recently been observed that the bone

tissue of these plates was rich in blood vessels, and that the plates in one row were staggered in relation to those in the second row. The hypothesis has been put forward that the stegosaur could heat or cool its blood, by arranging the plates so that they were perpendicular or parallel to the sun's rays. We have already seen this method of exploiting the sun's warmth in the *Edaphosaurus* (see the volume *Reptiles*, Chap. 12).

THE SMALL HEAD

Stegosaurs are also characterized by an incredibly small head in relation to the size of the rest of the body. For these herbivorous dinosaurs, the problem again arises of disproportion between the quantity of food necessary for the animal and the dimensions of the mouth. The small head contains an equally limited brain, so that these dinosaurs again exhibit enlargements of the spinal cord—especially at the junction of the hind limbs—which assist the insignificant brain.

Protoceratops

About 130 million years ago, the *Protoceratops* used to deposit their eggs in the Mongolian sands. The young were fully formed at hatching.

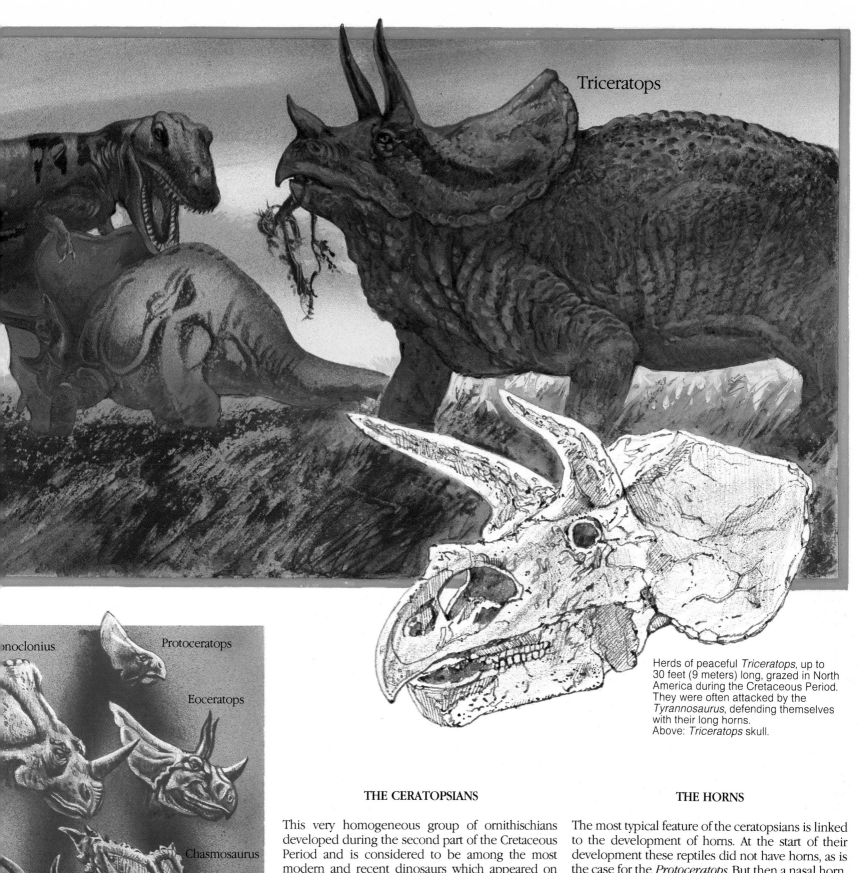

Triceratops

Herds of peaceful *Triceratops*, up to 30 feet (9 meters) long, grazed in North America during the Cretaceous Period. They were often attacked by the *Tyrannosaurus*, defending themselves with their long horns.
Above: *Triceratops* skull.

Protoceratops

noclonius

Eoceratops

Chasmosaurus

Styracosaurus

The evolution and increase in size of the horn in ceratopsians lasted for millions of years. Some of their bizarre forms are depicted here, reconstructed on the basis of numerous fossil finds.

THE CERATOPSIANS

This very homogeneous group of ornithischians developed during the second part of the Cretaceous Period and is considered to be among the most modern and recent dinosaurs which appeared on Earth. The ceratopsians probably had social inclinations: they lived in herds that roamed, grazing over the savannas and the grassy expanses of the high plateaux. Like all herbivores, the ceratopsians had enemies that threatened their existence, but a skull furnished with a bony extension that covered and protected a large part of the neck was developed and took on increasing importance.

THE HORNS

The most typical feature of the ceratopsians is linked to the development of horns. At the start of their development these reptiles did not have horns, as is the case for the *Protoceratops*. But then a nasal horn, similar to that of the rhinoceros, appeared. The *Styracosaurus* had a dozen horns making a charge by this animal particularly dangerous. One can imagine a struggle between a ceratopsian and a *Tyrannosaurus*, with the carnivore trying to sink its jaws into the soft parts of the herbivore, while the latter, shaking its head around, endeavored to attack and wound the aggressor. This is not pure fantasy, skeletal remains of large carnivores have been found with badly healed fractures of the pelvic bones and hind limbs, probably inflicted by powerful ceratopsians. At the end of the Cretaceous Period, close to the fateful date of extinction of the dinosaurs, the ceratopsians were the most common, especially in North America.

Skimming the water, the *Rhamphorhynchus* caught and held fish with its sharp teeth.
The tail ended in a lozenge-shaped rudder, used as a stabilizer in flight.

7. THE PTEROSAURS

This evolutionary line includes those reptiles which were the first to learn the technique of flight, although it was based on exploiting rising hot currents of air to launch themselves vertically down to the sea; in other words it was gliding flight. Their wings did not beat like birds or bats, but were limited to spreading out, both in order to utilize the upward thrust of the currents and in order to control direction. Despite this limitation, the pterosaurs achieved such ability in gliding flight that the most advanced forms reached enormous dimensions, with a wingspread of 49-55 feet (15-17 meters): the most gigantic creature that ever, through its own forces, left the ground to soar in the air.

From the features of the skull and teeth, the origin of pterosaurs from the techodont arcosaurs is evident, although no intermediate form between a reptile that walks and one that flies is known. Even the most ancient pterosaur presents characteristics suitable for flight, so that nothing is known of the origin of the wing, or rather of the patagium.

THEIR FLIGHT

The possibility of soaring in the air was furnished by a slender membrane that stretched from an enormously elongated toe, the fourth, to the side parts of the body. It was a patagium similar to that of the modern bats, although the reptile was not capable of beating its wings; the skeleton of the thoracic cage, where the muscle to perform this movement would have been inserted, was too slender and delicate. In addition the pelvis and hind paws were very small, so that it must be presumed that the pterosaurs walked with great difficulty. The first three toes of the forepaws and t[toes of the hind paws were furnished with stro claws, and it is supposed that these reptiles climb on trees or rocks to find the right place to laun themselves into space and then glide with their amp wings extended, ready to exploit the wind.

THEIR FOOD

According to one of the most widely held opinion these reptiles were skillful fishers of prey, which th seized in flight while skimming over the water. T variety of their dentition and the presence of fi bones found together with the remains of pterosau are factors supporting this hypothesis. Only the gia *Quetzalcoatlus* has been found a long way from t sea and near bones of dinosaurs, so it may be that the pterosaurs devoured carrion, rather like the prese day vultures. In any case, all of them had a skull and very sturdy neck that contrasted with the rest of t body, which was lighter and frailer. The pterosaurs split into two groups which may be related to ea other: the rhamphorhynchi and the pterodactyls.

14

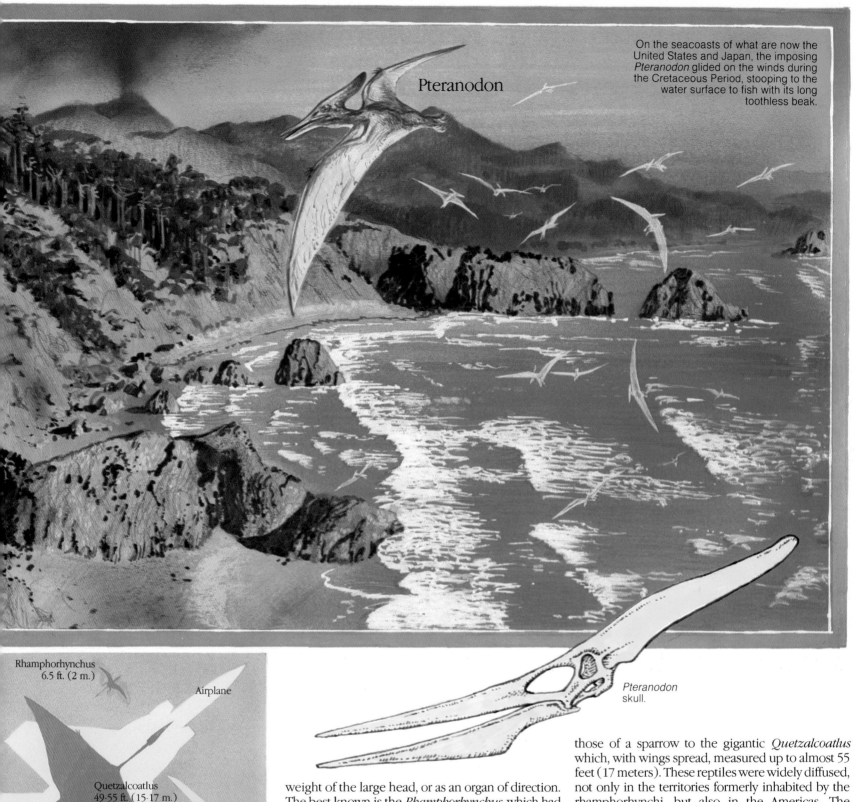

Pteranodon

On the seacoasts of what are now the United States and Japan, the imposing *Pteranodon* glided on the winds during the Cretaceous Period, stooping to the water surface to fish with its long toothless beak.

Pteranodon skull.

Rhamphorhynchus
6.5 ft. (2 m.)

Airplane

Quetzalcoatlus
49-55 ft. (15-17 m.)
estimated size

Pteranodon
26 ft. (8 m.)

The wingspans of three pterosaurs, compared with a middle-sized airplane.

THE RHAMPHORHYNCHI

They are among the oldest, but not the most primitive, since they lived and flew throughout the Jurassic Period, 135-180 million years ago. Small in size, with a wingspread not exceeding 31 inches (80 centimeters), they had a very long tail, perhaps to balance the weight of the large head, or as an organ of direction. The best known is the *Rhamphorhynchus*, which had a bulky head and a mouth armed with long, sharp teeth arranged irregularly; it lived in Europe and Africa. The rhamphorhynchi disappeared from the scene at the end of the Jurassic Period, perhaps because they were pursued by another group of pterosaurs in full expansion, the pterodactyls.

THE PTERODACTYLS

This group of flying reptiles also has a very long fourth toe on its forelimb in order to support the large patagium, but compared with the rhamphorhynchi it completely lacks a tail. Some, like the *Pteranodon*, have a broad crest on the skull, perhaps in order to balance the very long snout or as an organ of direction. Among the pterodactyls we find a great variety of specimens, with dimensions ranging from those of a sparrow to the gigantic *Quetzalcoatlus* which, with wings spread, measured up to almost 55 feet (17 meters). These reptiles were widely diffused, not only in the territories formerly inhabited by the rhamphorhynchi, but also in the Americas. The pterodactyls died out at the same time as the dinosaurs, 65 million years ago—a fatal date for all the dominant reptiles.

AN ASTOUNDING DETAIL

In the fossilized rock discoveries of some pterosaurs, alongside the bones, the clear imprint has been left of numerous hairs covering the animals' skin. This discovery aroused a great deal of talk, as hair had previously been looked upon as a characteristic exclusive to mammals. The presence of hairs on the body of a reptile strengthens the present-day hypothesis that many of them, the dominators of the Secondary Era, were capable of conserving body heat, and, hence, were something more than the existing reptiles which do not possess this important capacity.

BIOLOGICAL CAUSES

Death by specialization

Change in plants

Dinosaurs were stupid

Dinosaurs were cold

Eggshells became thinner

Only males were born

Only females were born

Poisoning by plants

Inbreeding

Predation of eggs
by mammals

Endocrine malfunctions

Diseases

8. THE DEATH OF THE DINOSAURS: BIOLOGICAL CAUSES

At the end of the Secondary Era, 65 million years ago, all the ruling reptiles, especially the dinosaurs, died out and disappeared. The phenomenon is so unusual in the history of evolution that it arouses strong interest. Researchers began to investigate the cause of the spectacular extinction of the dinosaurs, and dozens of hypotheses have been accumulated, testifying to the uncertainty still existing in relation to this problem. Of the many set out in the table illustrated above, only those most likely or most reliable will be discussed.

DEATH THROUGH SPECIALIZATION

This is one of the most fascinating hypotheses, largely because of the implications that can be derived from it. When an environment remains constant for a long time, as happened in the Secondary Era, the animals that live in it tend to perfect their characteristics, adapting them ever more closely to the necessities of the habitat. If this happens, the animal becomes more specialized and therefore more efficient, but it loses flexibility so that the onset of a variation in the environment leads to its extinction. The giant herbivorous dinosaurs had to have sufficiently deep areas of water available to support the weight of their bulky bodies, but if the level of the water changed, due to prolonged drought or copious rainfall, the

dinosaur was doomed. The climate, which had remained stable during the Secondary Era, changed at the beginning of the Tertiary Era, and, although not the only one, this is probably the most significant cause of the extinction of those dinosaurs that were highly specialized.

THE PLANTS CHANGE

Toward the end of the Secondary Era there was a radical change in vegetation: the angiosperms, the most common vegetable forms in our day, appeared and became widespread, bringing new characteristics. It is likely that the herbivorous dinosaurs were not capable of adapting themselves to the new food, so they became extinct, together with the carnivores that

Some examples of the hypothetical biological causes of the extinction of the dinosaurs. **1**) Death by specialization: a change in climate dried up the swamps and lakes that supported the enormous weight of the largest dinosaurs. **2**) A change in vegetation: the new angiosperms, including magnolias and conifers, were not suited to nutrition of herbivorous dinosaurs. **3**) The dinosaurs were stupid: yet there were dinosaurs like the *Stenonychosaurus* that had a well-developed brain. **4**) It became too cold for the dinosaurs: yet several species regulated their body heat and were covered with fur. **5**) The thickness of their eggshells diminished, preventing the embryos from completing their development.

16

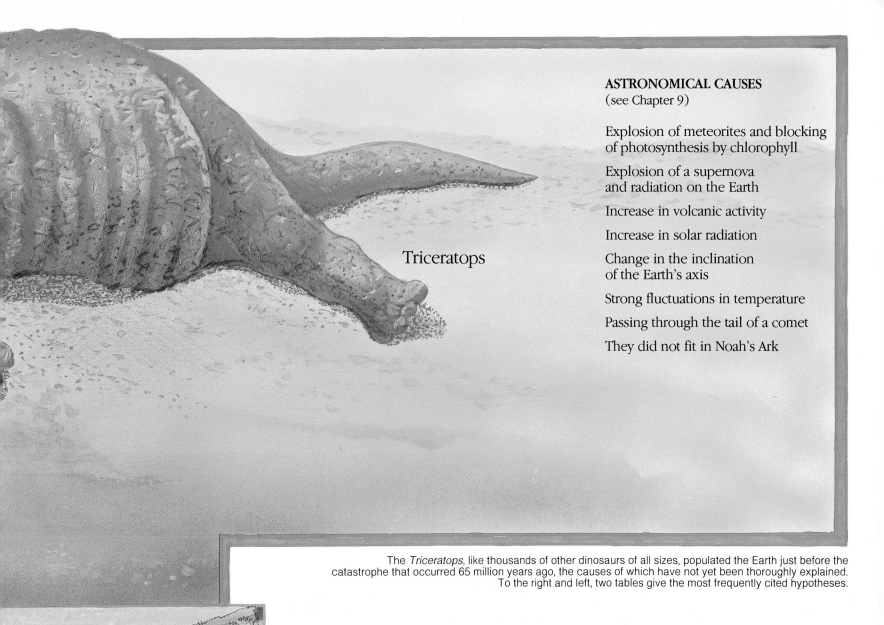

Triceratops

ASTRONOMICAL CAUSES
(see Chapter 9)

Explosion of meteorites and blocking
of photosynthesis by chlorophyll

Explosion of a supernova
and radiation on the Earth

Increase in volcanic activity

Increase in solar radiation

Change in the inclination
of the Earth's axis

Strong fluctuations in temperature

Passing through the tail of a comet

They did not fit in Noah's Ark

The *Triceratops*, like thousands of other dinosaurs of all sizes, populated the Earth just before the catastrophe that occurred 65 million years ago, the causes of which have not yet been thoroughly explained. To the right and left, two tables give the most frequently cited hypotheses.

preyed on them. This is a probable cause, even if it does not explain everything, since some of the most modern dinosaurs, such as the *Triceratops*, probably already fed on grass as we know it today.

THE STUPID DINOSAUR

Competition between the slow dinosaur with a small brain and the more agile and intelligent mammal has also been suggested. But this hypothesis has been dropped since the discovery of dinosaurs, such as dromeosaurs, with very bulky brains and light skeletons, factors which lead us to expect considerable ability and competitiveness. Unfortunately even the "intelligent" dinosaurs perished when the fatal day arrived.

THE DINOSAUR IS COLD

Another hypothesis that enjoyed wide credit until a few years ago emphasizes the great change in climate that occurred simultaneously with the extinction of the dinosaurs. The constant dry heat which had characterized the Secondary Era, favoring the development and expansion of reptiles, notoriously lovers of warmth, was followed by a colder period and an alternation of seasons. This climate caused slaughter among the dinosaurs, which were unable to

withstand the cold or, in any case, changes in temperature. In the light of more recent studies, this hypothesis has proved rather weak. Today, the idea that the dinosaurs were able to thermoregulate their bodies is gaining ground and there is evidence to support this. The imprint of hair in the case of pterosaurs, for example, indicates that they had fur to protect them from the cold; in addition, the properties of the bone tissue of many dinosaurs are almost identical with those of mammals and profoundly different from those of any living reptile, thus indicating a very active metabolism capable even of producing heat. The dinosaur was probably able to thermoregulate itself and could, consequently, overcome the difficulties of low temperature.

THE THICKNESS OF EGGS

A precise and accurate statistical investigation of the thickness of the shells of dinosaur eggs indicates that they became progressively thinner, with a big increase in fragility. However, many reptiles of the Secondary Era were ovoviparous, giving birth to offspring that were already efficient and independent, but even these reptiles perished.

In conclusion, there is no single biological cause that can explain everything; there was perhaps a conjunction of negative events that led to extinction.

The Frenchman Georges Cuvier was one of the founders of paleontology. He analyzed and classified fossil and living molluscs, fish, mammals and reptiles.

9. THE DEATH OF THE DINOSAURS: ASTRONOMICAL CAUSES

METEORITES

Cuvier, the late nineteenth century naturalist, was the first person to have recourse to "catastrophic" hypotheses to explain the sudden disappearance of many animal forms, even though at the time little was known about the possibility of an impact of celestial bodies with the Earth. On hot summer nights we have all seen "shooting stars" rapidly furrow the sky. The phenomenon occurs when the Earth in its orbit approaches swarms of cosmic material, which it attracts to itself through the force of gravity. Most of this material is too small to reach our planet and is burnt up as soon as it enters the atmosphere, leaving the characteristic incandescent wake. On very rare occasions, however, it may happen that larger bodies—meteorites—succeed in reaching the Earth: on impact they explode, making large craters. On the basis of this phenomenon some scientists have seen meteorites as bearing the main responsibility for the death of the dinosaurs.

A DISCONCERTING DISCOVERY

In 1977, the American geologist Walter Alvarez, when analyzing a sediment layer of cretaceous limestone about 65 million years old, near Gubbio, Italy, discovered that the concentration of iridium, a very rare element, was incredibly high. In 1980, with the help of his father, Luis, a Nobel-prize-winning physicist, he propounded the hypothesis of the impact on Earth of a huge meteorite, the explosion of which released a cloud of dust, containing iridium

among other things, which blocked sunlight from the Earth's surface. First to die were the plants—totally dependent on the Sun for photosynthesis—followed along a logical food chain by the herbivore and then the carnivore dinosaurs. The hypothesis was sensational, exciting chiefly those not directly involved in this branch of research, but leaving paleontologists and biologists skeptical.

In 1983, a paleontologist at Chicago University, John Sepkoski, and some of his colleagues, after a long statistical investigation of the presence and disappearance of species in the last 250 million years, observed that the extermination of the dinosaurs was not the only dramatic event in the history of life on

Above: Arizona's Barringer Meteorite Crater, punched out some 50,000 years ago by a meteorite, is 550 feet (170 meters) deep, and 3,900 feet (1,200 meters) across.

Top: the explosion of a meteorite may have been the cause of a cloud of iridium whose deposits (discovered in Italy by Walter Alvarez in 1977) blocked photosynthesis in chlorophyll.

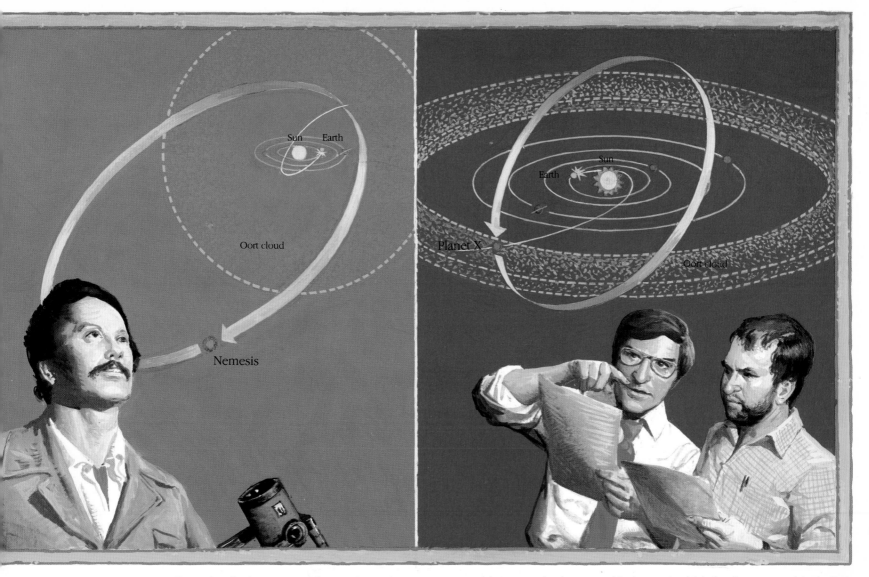

Recently scientists suggested a new theory that attempts to explain mass extinctions—notably the one in which the dinosaurs perished—that periodically punctuate the history of our planet. Every 26 million years, the theory holds, a dim star companion to the Sun (Nemesis), or a mysterious tenth planet in our system (Planet X) in their elliptical orbit (yellow) are believed to intersect the Oort cloud of comets surrounding the solar system, gravitationally hurling some of them toward Earth. The impact spews enough debris into the atmosphere to block the sunlight for months. As the skies darken, temperature on the ground plummets and the majority of existing plant and animal species die. R. Muller (on the left) is the American physicist responsible for the Nemesis theory. The theory of Planet X was devised by Louisiana's astrophysicists J. Matese and D. Whitmire (on the right).

rth. Regularly, every 26 million years, an event leads a hecatomb of living forms. The catastrophe that sulted in extinction of the dinosaurs was not a ance fact, but predictable and will be repeated. The st catastrophe occurred 11 million years ago, and the ext one will take place in 15 million years. It now mained to discover the cause of this precise and ethodical event, clearly of astronomical origin. Two potheses enjoy a certain amount of credit.

THE NEMESIS HYPOTHESIS

nis hypothesis blames Oort's Cloud, a swarm of one llion astral bodies that envelops our solar system. In ormal conditions, this enormous mass of cosmic aterial revolves calmly and harmlessly. But, at tervals of millions of years, the Sun's "dim ompanion"—a star that has been postulated by the lifornian physicist Richard Muller—in its enormous liptical orbit approaches Oort's Cloud and through e action of its gravity tears away an uncertain umber of astral bodies destined to fall on the Sun, or its planets, including Earth which is bombarded by eteorites, some of them huge, with the consequences ready described. The Sun's dim companion star, hich has never been seen, has been called Nemesis.

THE PLANET X HYPOTHESIS

The astrophysicists John Matese and Daniel Whitmire, on the other hand, believe that the disturbance of Oort's Cloud is due to the tenth planet in our solar system. This has never been observed directly either and is termed Planet X. The existence of this planet is perhaps more likely, as it may be the cause of the anomalies in Neptune's orbit. Planet X completes its enormous orbit roughly every 56 million years, intersecting Oort's Cloud twice in every orbit and thus causing the detachment of many meteorites, inexorably destined to be captured by the solar system.

SKEPTICISM

These researches, conducted with the utmost care by authoritative scientists in qualified laboratories, are clearly impressive, but scientific circles are still doubtful about the hypothesis of a block of chlorophyll synthesis—an event of this kind could not confine its effect to only some large groups of animals. In fact, according to paleontological investigations, 65 million years ago dinosaurs, flying reptiles, and marine reptiles became extinct among

the vertebrates and ammonites among the invertebrates, but there is no trace of crisis among birds, plants, or teleostean fish, which were actually in full expansion during that period.

A CURIOUS HYPOTHESIS

Among the many hypotheses put forward, there is also the one proposed by the American neocreationists, who, interpreting the words of the Bible literally, believe that the dinosaurs could not enter Noah's ark owing to their size and hence were drowned. It is a hypothesis like many others, but as it takes its origin from a precise ideological axiom, leaves no space for discussion.

THE DINOSAURS' RELATIONS

Sixty-five million years ago all the dinosaurs disappeared, but there are some people who believe it is remotely possible that in the depths of tropical forests difficult to explore there are surviving species of this great group of reptiles. It cannot be excluded *a priori*, but if there are survivors they will not be the huge animals we all might expect but much less striking and spectacular creatures.

Archaeopteryx

Swept out to sea by a storm, two *Archaeopteryx* were drowned and then fossilized in the sediments of a lagoon. Right: a fossil of *Archaeopteryx* (Solnhofen, Germany).

10. ORIGIN OF BIRDS

THE FIRST BIRD

Toward the end of the Jurassic Period, about 140-150 million years ago, in a lagoon in the present-day Bavaria (Germany), a furious thunderstorm broke out with lightning, downpours of water, and winds that bent the trees. Two animals, not very expert at flying, attempted desperately to withstand the forces unleashed by nature, but the inexorable wind carried

them off the shore and they were drowned. Their carcasses fell to the bottom of the lagoon, and the silt brought down by the rivers in spate quickly covered them. The sediment was then consolidated into rock, a limestone of exceptionally fine grain, at one time used as stone for printing, i.e. lithographic. These fortunate circumstances, combined with the fact that whoever excavated these rocks and found the skeleton of one of these animals understood the

importance of the discovery, resulted in the specimen being preserved. In this precious fossil, together with the well-preserved skeleton, the clear imprints of the feathers that adorned the body can be discerned. The animal was thus a bird, the most ancient bird that known today. Subsequently, in these same Bavaria deposits of Solnhofen, a second specimen came t light, again in an excellent state of preservation. If on considers the rarity of fossil skeletons of bird

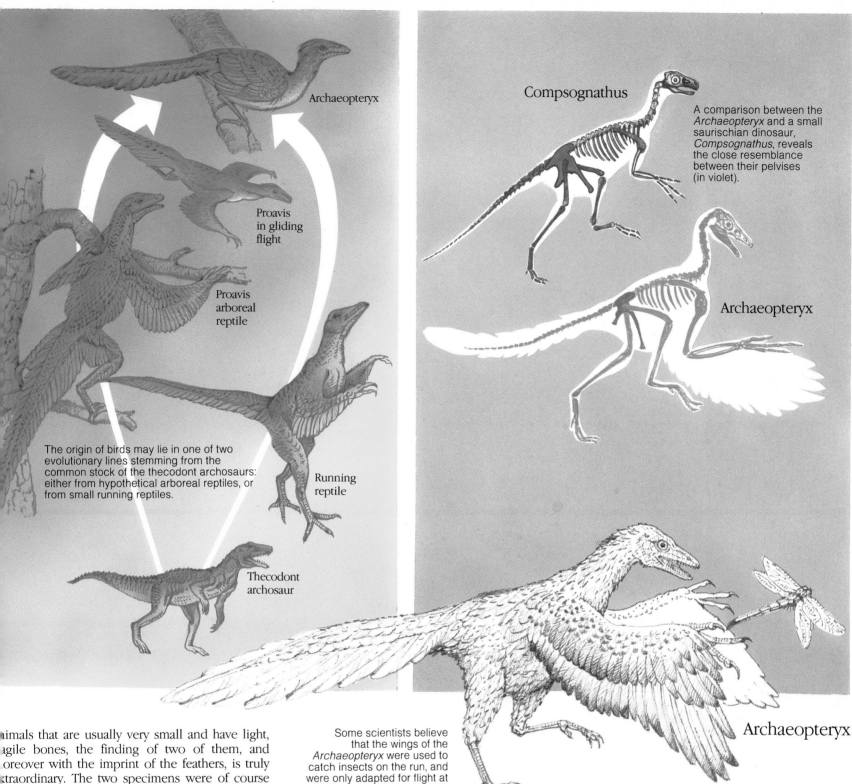

Archaeopteryx

Proavis
in gliding
flight

Proavis
arboreal
reptile

The origin of birds may lie in one of two
evolutionary lines stemming from the
common stock of the thecodont archosaurs:
either from hypothetical arboreal reptiles, or
from small running reptiles.

Running
reptile

Thecodont
archosaur

Compsognathus

A comparison between the
Archaeopteryx and a small
saurischian dinosaur,
Compsognathus, reveals
the close resemblance
between their pelvises
(in violet).

Archaeopteryx

Archaeopteryx

Some scientists believe
that the wings of the
Archaeopteryx were used to
catch insects on the run, and
were only adapted for flight at
a later stage.

imals that are usually very small and have light,
agile bones, the finding of two of them, and
moreover with the imprint of the feathers, is truly
extraordinary. The two specimens were of course
studied and received a name. *Archaeopteryx* means
"ancient wing," and *lithographica* is derived from the
zone in which they were found—lithographic
limestone. A study of the birds' skeletons immediately
showed that the principal characteristics were
typically reptilian, with the exception of the forked
avicula.

THE INTERMEDIATE FORM

In the polemics raised by the theories of evolution,
one of the anti-evolutionists' principal arguments is
the absence of intermediate forms between the great
classes; in other words, there are no living lizards with
fur or mammary glands that are forerunners of the
mammal, nor crocodiles with wings. But if this is true
for living forms, it is by no means the case for those
that are extinct. In the volume *Reptiles* we saw that the
periodont therapsids forerun or are already mammals;

it now clearly emerges that the *Archaeopteryx* is an
intermediate form. Today, in view of the wings and
the imprints of feathers, nobody doubts that this
specimen is a bird, but if the two fossils had been
preserved in a rock of coarser grain, unsuitable for
retaining the imprint of the feathers, everybody would
have agreed on classifying these animals among the
thecodont reptiles, or among the saurischian
dinosaurs, which they greatly resemble.

ORIGIN OF FEATHERS

In the study of the development of feathers, it was
observed that the first stages of growth of this structure
are entirely similar to those of the development of
scales; hence, it would seem to be a logical deduction

that the feather is an ultraspecialized scale. Perhaps
the first feathers appeared on the bodies of reptiles to
protect them from the cold; we have already seen that
the most evolved dinosaurs probably had warm blood
and required protection against dispersion of body
heat. Only in a later phase was there development
from the protective feather to the feather adapted for
flight. In this connection, two hypotheses are put
forward. According to the first, the wing progressively
developed in tree-climbing saurischian reptiles who,
leaping from one branch to another, found
increasingly good support in longer and longer
feathers. The other hypothesis considers that the
progenitors of the birds were running reptiles, and
that the *Archaeopteryx* was itself a runner; what we
look upon as a wing to fly was a device to capture
insects better during running. But the hypothesis that
earns the most credit is the one that sees the
Archaeopteryx as a flying animal.

21

11. EXTINCT BIRDS

Archaeopteryx

ARCHAEOPTERYX

The first true bird that appeared on Earth was, as we saw in the last chapter, the *Archaeopteryx lithographica*, which lived in Europe 140-150 million years ago.

This ancient specimen, about as big as a crow, could not have been a good flier: the breast muscles were weak, the paws sturdy, and the long tail must have caused considerable trouble during flight. We already know that running dinosaurs with erect posture were characterized by a powerful tail, and it cannot, therefore, be excluded that the *Archaeopteryx* was an agile runner, although the three strong claws on the forepaw toes indicate that it could climb trees and rocks. Perhaps it had learnt to fly by gliding on wings and tail. Despite the characteristics of extreme primitiveness, the *Archaeopteryx* is classified among the birds.

THE ORNITHURIANS

A long interval of time separates the remains of the *Archaeopteryx* from those of other birds that were next to appear on the scene some 80-90 million years ago. During this long interval, about which we know nothing, the fundamental characteristics of the class were being perfected, and we shall see that they remained practically unchanged in all birds combined in the subclass of ornithurians. This subclass is split into odontognaths (ancient birds still furnished with teeth), paleognaths (birds that renounced flight in order to concentrate on running), and neognaths (flying birds in a broad sense).

THE ODONTOGNATHS

The primitiveness of the odontognaths is evidenced by the presence in the beak of small, sharp, conical teeth, a typical reptilian characteristic. They were the last birds to have teeth. After them, the beak definitely has the advantage and teeth disappear completely. The scene in which the odontognaths appear is varied: the *Archaeopteryx* flew—if it flew—in Europe during the Jurassic Period; the odontognaths flew in North America. More precisely, their skeletons have been found in late cretaceous deposits in Kansas, but as they were already evolved birds, it may be expected that they were much more widespread.

The most widely accepted hypothesis about the behavior of this ancient bird, which was the size of a crow, considers the *Archaeopteryx* to have been a glider that climbed onto tree trunks or rocks and then launched itself into gliding flight, with wing and tail feathers fully extended.

Ichthyornis

Hesperornis

HESPERORNIS

Those expecting to find primitive characteristics in this ancient bird are grossly mistaken, as the *Hesperornis* exhibits a strong specialization for the aquatic life. We are not looking at an ancient animal that evolved in order to acquire the characteristics of the new class, but at a creature that has deviated from the natural habitat in order to colonize a new environment. The phenomenon is not new, we have already seen that both amphibians and reptiles originated forms that returned to the water and took on characteristics adapted to swimming. But those forms appeared when the two classes were in full expansion, while the *Hesperornis*, as far as we know, is one of the most ancient birds. Our knowledge of the origin of birds and their diffusion is greatly lacking, as the two known specimens of odontognaths already have an advanced organization.

The *Hesperornis*, in fact, renounced the typical prerogatives of the bird, since it did not fly, but swam. Indeed, its wings were actually reduced to small stumps, with a small and insignificant residual humerus. This peculiarity gives rise to perplexities: the disappearance of the forelimb must have taken a long time, measurable in tens of millions of years, about which we know nothing. The *Hesperornis* swam with the sturdy hind paws rather far back on the bust. The considerable size of this first swimming bird could reach 70 inches (180 centimeters). When it was obliged to go ashore in order to lay eggs, it must have walked very badly, with little jumps, rather like penguins do today; but this ancient bird's kingdom was the sea, where it passed the greater part of its time in pursuit of fish, which it caught with its long bill armed with teeth.

ICHTHYORNIS

While the *Hesperornis* swam in the lagoons of Kansas, a bird no larger than a pigeon, the *Ichthyornis*, flew in the air. Its primitiveness is shown only by the presence of teeth, otherwise it was similar to modern birds. The wing skeleton was already well formed, and the breast-bone with the robust sternum gives reason to suppose it had powerful muscles for flying: the animal was already capable of beating its wings strongly and exceeding all the limitations of gliding flight. The *Ichthyornis* was already a true bird, although with a still somewhat primitive skull.

About 90 million years ago, in North America, there were two bird species far more evolved than the *Archaeopteryx*: the *Hesperornis regalis* was specialized for swimming, with almost total loss of the forelimbs; the *Ichthyornis victor*, on the other hand, was an excellent flier.

MODERN BIRDS

The *Ichthyornis* and the *Hesperornis* as we saw in the previous chapter are, together with the *Archaeopteryx*, the only known birds that lived in the Secondary Era and dwelt on the Earth with the dinosaurs. But, in view of the greatly advanced and evolved characteristics, especially of the first two species, it seems logical to suppose that during that Era the class of birds was already in full expansion and already possessed the anatomical and functional characteristics that distinguish it.

Unfortunately, however, for the first few million years of this class's existence our paleontological knowledge is absolutely inadequate and does not offer a full history of the origin of birds, but only short, isolated flashes. The reason for this may lie in the particular lightness of the skeleton of these animals, which is difficult to fossilize, and in their habits of life. Already when speaking of fossilization (Chap. 1), we saw that a small organism living in forests is unlikely to find ideal conditions for its fossilization. Life in the bush, where the carcass would fall, is too abundant, and everything is rapidly destroyed or rather reused. We know the *Archaeopteryx* because two specimens fell into a lagoon and we have 50 fossil skeletons of *Hesperornis* available, as they were sea birds—both species were thus in the best conditions to be fossilized. But how many species of birds were living with the huge dinosaurs during the Secondary Era? It is impossible to attempt any reply, but certainly some hundreds, perhaps thousands, as the *Ichthyornis* and *Hesperornis* were already very advanced in their evolution and profoundly different from each other.

THE RAMIFICATIONS OF THE CLASS

In the classes examined in the previous volumes of this series it was possible to draw up what is known as a "phylogenetic tree," in order to clarify the succession of the different orders and the degree of relationship between families; this is not possible for birds, except in very broad outline. The class is very homogeneous in complexity of characteristics, but when an evolutionary branch is distinguished by some peculiarity (running birds, for example, who have rejected flight) there can be no certainty about where it originated. The result is that either the different orders are set out, one separate from the other (as we see in the final endpaper), or a tree is drawn up with many question marks and few branches.

CHARACTERISTICS OF THE CLASS

A bird, like any other vertebrate, has the typical organs and apparatuses of its class—a brain, an intestine, two lungs, a skeleton, etc.—but highly evolved and specialized. The basic characteristics are typically reptilian, and, in fact, the class derives directly from the saurischian dinosaurs, but with its own particular, advanced acquisitions. The causes that have led to this evolution may be sought both in specialization for

The problem of finding relationships between the different forms of birds today has not yet been reliably solved and hence the genealogical tree of this class is full of question marks.

flight and in solution of the problems connected with thermoregulation. Birds, like mammals, have a thermoregulated body, or in other words they keep their temperature constant even if the outside environment is hotter or colder. In previous chapters and in the volume *Reptiles* we have seen that the possibility of thermoregulating the body may even have appeared among reptiles—both in the theriodont therapsids (mammal-like reptiles) and in the dinosaurs, as well as in the pterosaurs (flying reptiles)—but this is only supposition based on certain characteristics of the skeleton. In birds and mammals, on the other hand, thermoregulation is a basic characteristic, but one that required many devices to achieve.

WHY THERMOREGULATION?

The body temperature of a fish, an amphibian, or a reptile living in our time is at the mercy of the environmental temperature; if this rises or drops, the body heat follows the same variations (fish, amphibians, and reptiles are thus cold-blooded or

heterothermal). When the weather is too cold or too hot, the animal must endeavor to escape from the unfavorable conditions by hiding in deep lairs or by becoming lethargic and slowing down all the functions of its organism. A warm-blooded or homeotherm animal, on the other hand, keeps its temperature constant at all times and can perform all vital processes even in unfavorable environmental conditions. The first advantage of the homeotherm over the heterotherm is the ability to live at low or high temperatures. The second, and no less important, advantage is linked to the increase in metabolism that is obtained at high temperatures. A biochemical law establishes a ratio between metabolism and body temperature; the higher the latter, the more the metabolism is increased so that the animal becomes more lively, quicker in its reactions, more sensitive, and more rapid in all its functions. The advantages are clear, but homeothermy imposes the solution to a variety of problems, as we shall see later, which the two classes, birds and mammals, will face and resolve with different solutions.

House sparrow

female

male

Map: in red the house sparrow's original range; in pink the subsequent expansions to the various continents.

North America

South America

Europe

Asia

Africa

Australia

THERMOREGULATION

Birds are thermoregulated at about 106° F (41° C), mammals at 98.6° F (37° C). The problems linked to thermoregulation are complex. The animal must produce heat, since the temperature of the environment is generally lower than that of the body, but to do this it is necessary to eat much more, digest more quickly, and absorb more oxygen from the air as the metabolism of the entire organism is higher. The body must also be protected from heat loss, which is greater the colder the environment. Lastly a cooling system is necessary when the outside temperature is higher than that of the body, as well as a thermal control unit that is capable of starting and stopping the different cooling and heating systems.

The house sparrow is a good example of thermoregulation in view of its ability to adapt to the most varied climates and hence to a wide range of foods with which to meet its energy requirements. As a result of this capacity it has succeeded in colonizing all the continents, except the Antarctic. In the wake of the European peoples it has spread far beyond its original area, even to islands hundreds of miles from the mainland. During the winter it retains heat by puffing up its feathers and, when food is scarce, by reducing its activity to the bare minimum in order to avoid energy and heat losses; its behavior is the complete opposite in the summer, when the temperature is higher and there is much more food available.

A HIBERNATING BIRD

There is only one bird capable of bringing about a reduction in its temperature, so as to fall into a state of lethargy for months at a time, as mammals do. This is the North American poorwill, which passes the winter in natural hollows, lowering its body temperature from 107 to 68 °F (42 to 20 °C). Only a few other birds, such as swifts, hummingbirds and mousebirds, have the same capacity, and then only for a limited time, or only at night.

Poorwill

Below and right: side and rear view of a rock dove showing the internal arrangement of the respiratory organs.

trachea

lung

air sac

parabronchus

mesobronchus

trachea

lung

air sac

Left: diagram of lung. The flow of air through a bird's respiratory apparatus is highly complicated. Oxygen from the air sacs passes into the mesobronchus and then into the parabronchi, where it is absorbed by the blood.

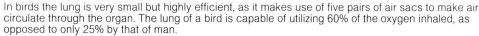

In birds the lung is very small but highly efficient, as it makes use of five pairs of air sacs to make air circulate through the organ. The lung of a bird is capable of utilizing 60% of the oxygen inhaled, as opposed to only 25% by that of man.

At one time the death by asphyxiation of a canary in a cage warned miners of dangerous concentrations of firedamp.

13. HOW THEY BREATHE AND HOW THEY EAT

When people clear a rabbit of entrails before cooking it, they also remove the large and bulky lungs that are enclosed in the thoracic cage; when they perform the same operation with a fowl, they cannot remove the lungs; they are small and thrust between the vertebrae of the spinal column and can hardly be seen. In view of the extreme smallness of their lungs, it might be thought that birds do not require much oxygen to live. Nothing could be further from the truth.

METABOLISM

Metabolism is a complex process on the basis of which changes occur in living creatures from one type of energy (for example, the chemical energy of foods), to another type of energy (for example, heat or movement). As we have seen, birds have a basic temperature of about 106 °F (41 °C). But, we repeat, to obtain this temperature a great deal of energy is

required, which means a lot of food has to be digested quickly and well. Then, when the absorbed organic substances reach the tissues, in order to obtain heat from them, a great deal of oxygen is necessary to oxidize them. Birds have a higher metabolism than mammals. In addition, as they are generally small animals, they lose more heat. Hence, birds have an average oxygen consumption up to 20 times greater than that of mammals. And yet, they have lungs of very limited size in comparison with the rest of the body. How is this possible?

AN EXCEPTIONAL ORGAN: THE LUNG

In the lungs of amphibians, reptiles, and mammals air passes through the windpipe and bronchial tubes into the respiratory alveoli—where it remains for a varying amount of time in order to give up the oxygen to the blood and receive the carbon dioxide from the

blood—then it leaves, following the same route reverse. In this case, the exchange between the tw fluids (air and blood) cannot exceed 50%; if, in oth words, there are 100 parts of oxygen in the air, 50 w pass into the blood and 50 will remain unused (this in theory, in practice, for different reasons, much le oxygen passes into the blood). In birds, the lungs a built to overcome this loss, using numerous air sacs which no respiratory exchanges occur, but whic serve to make the air follow a very precise route. Th air penetrates the large abdominal air sac and fro there it is driven through the lung where it ca exchange the gases with blood and then procee further, reaching other air sacs that will expel the use air. Through this device, the efficiency of the lu rises to more than 60-65% of oxygen used from t total inhaled (against 20-25% in humans), th allowing the bird's requirements to be met witho recourse to excessively bulky structures. On

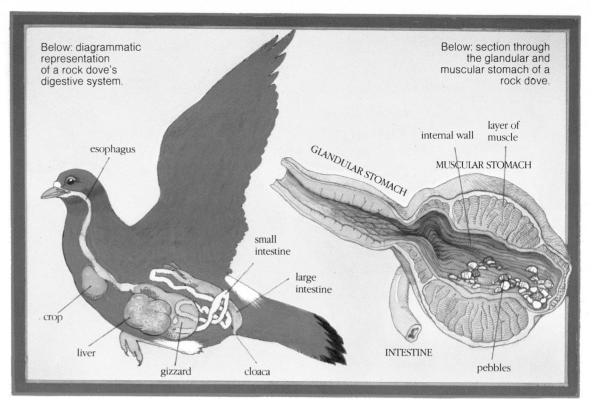

Below: diagrammatic representation of a rock dove's digestive system.

Below: section through the glandular and muscular stomach of a rock dove.

esophagus

small intestine

large intestine

crop

liver

gizzard

cloaca

GLANDULAR STOMACH

MUSCULAR STOMACH

internal wall

layer of muscle

INTESTINE

pebbles

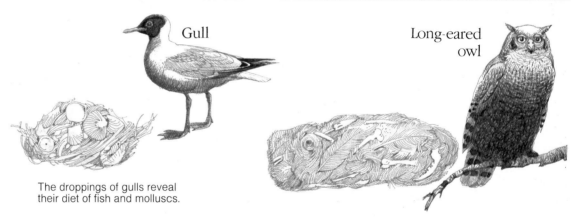

Gull

The droppings of gulls reveal their diet of fish and molluscs.

Long-eared owl

Nocturnal birds of prey, such as owls, expel droppings containing the hair and bones of the rodents that make up the major part of their diet.

American robin

Rock dove

Nearly all birds quench their thirst by dipping their beaks in the water, filling the mouth, tilting the head back so the water runs down their throat, and repeating these movements several times. Rock doves on the other hand drink by dipping the beak in the water and sucking.

recently have researchers succeeded in understanding something about how the lungs work in birds, but miners, up to a short time ago, were well aware of the great capabilities of this organ. They used to take a cage with a little bird underground, if there were exhalations of "firedamp" the first to feel them was the bird which, through its highly efficient lungs, quickly absorbed the deadly gas and by its death enabled the miners to escape in time.

BIRDS MASTICATE WITH THE STOMACH

In order to keep body temperature constant it is necessary to supply the organism with many organic substances to be burnt for the purpose of obtaining energy. A homeothermal animal not only must eat more, but must also digest more quickly in order to ensure a continuous supply of energy to its organism. Digestion is accelerated by masticating, which means reducing the food to small fragments so that the digestive enzymes break it down more quickly. Mammals, which are also homeothermal, masticate or

chew with the mouth, where the premolar or molar teeth are specialized for this purpose. Birds, on the other hand, masticate with the stomach. The digestive apparatus of birds is specialized to accelerate digestion as much as possible. In the case of grain-eating birds, the food is first stored in a sac in the esophagus (crop), from which it is taken in small portions and sent to a first, glandular stomach that enriches it with digestive enzymes. From there, it passes to a muscular stomach (or gizzard) where it is thoroughly chopped up by the muscular layers of the walls and the presence of small stones. From this second stomach, only a semiliquid product emerges and then continues into the middle intestine where digestion continues and absorption of the organic substances starts. In some birds, what cannot be reduced to mush in the muscular stomach (feathers, stones, hair, hoof, bones) is rejected to the outside; this is the so-called "droppings." The method is highly efficient: the bird swallows the food it manages to find, and later, in the safety of its nest, does it break it down in the stomach and send it to be digested.

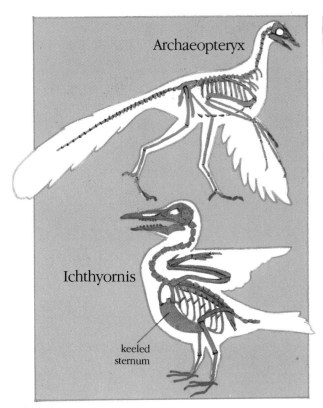

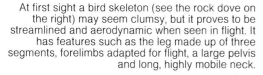

The skeleton of the *Archaeopteryx* still had many typical reptilian features, but the *Ichthyornis* already had distinctive characteristics exclusive to birds that can fly well, including the keel breastbone onto which the muscles that move the wings are attached.

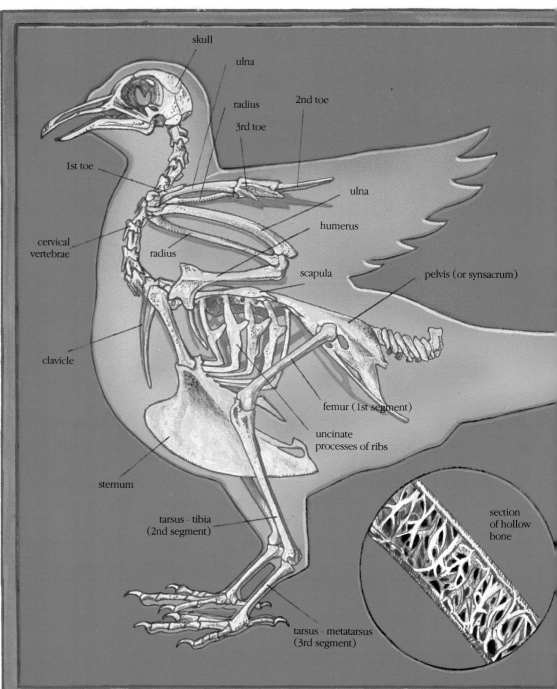

At first sight a bird skeleton (see the rock dove on the right) may seem clumsy, but it proves to be streamlined and aerodynamic when seen in flight. It has features such as the leg made up of three segments, forelimbs adapted for flight, a large pelvis and long, highly mobile neck.

14. THE SKELETON

Even a non-expert would, after short practice, be able to recognize a bird bone from that of any other vertebrate; it is sufficient in fact to weigh it in your hand: a bird bone is extraordinarily light, even in the case of bone that must support large loads, like those of the legs.

BONES FULL OF AIR

This lightness is due to the fact that in the bone tissue there are small air-filled cavities communicating with the air sacs. In the other vertebrates the bone is more compact and heavier, even where it is composed of spongy tissue. The skeleton of a bird is exceptionally light, a fundamental requirement for an animal that must soar in flight; it has been calculated that for the

same volume the bone of a bird weighs a third less than the bone of a mammal.

THE LEG

Although it may seem strange, the hind limb of birds has evolved for jumping; when the animal takes flight, albeit with certain exceptions, it must make an upward spring to allow the wings to make the first beat. In addition, when the animal lands, it stops more or less abruptly and the weight of its body and its speed suddenly come to bear on its limbs, which are obliged to absorb the shock. To meet all these requirements, part of the trunk vertebrae is fused with the large pelvis into a single piece, the synsacrum. But it is above all the hind limb that is modified. In the volume *Amphibians* in this series (Chap. 18) we already saw that in the hind limb of a frog a further articulated segment is formed in order to increase thrust for the leap (rather as though an extra spiral were added to a spring). The hind limb of birds likewise has three articulated segments which

originated through complicated procedures, which in brief achieve the same purpose. The fo thus rests on the ground with the toe phalanges or which vary in number from two, as in ostriches, to t normal four.

THE WING

The forelimb is also modified, in order to adapt its for flight: the segments become longer and from t extension of two toes a typical crushed ring bone formed and is located almost at the end of the wing There is also a small but functional first toe whi supports a tiny wing, the alula, with precise tasks. T pectoral girdle, onto which the wings are articulat is powerful in order to transmit the thrust original by flight to the entire skeleton; the two clavicles fused at one end and form a forked bo (characteristic of all birds), commonly known as t "wishbone" (which is often pulled between t people, the one left with the longer piece making wish that is supposed to come true).

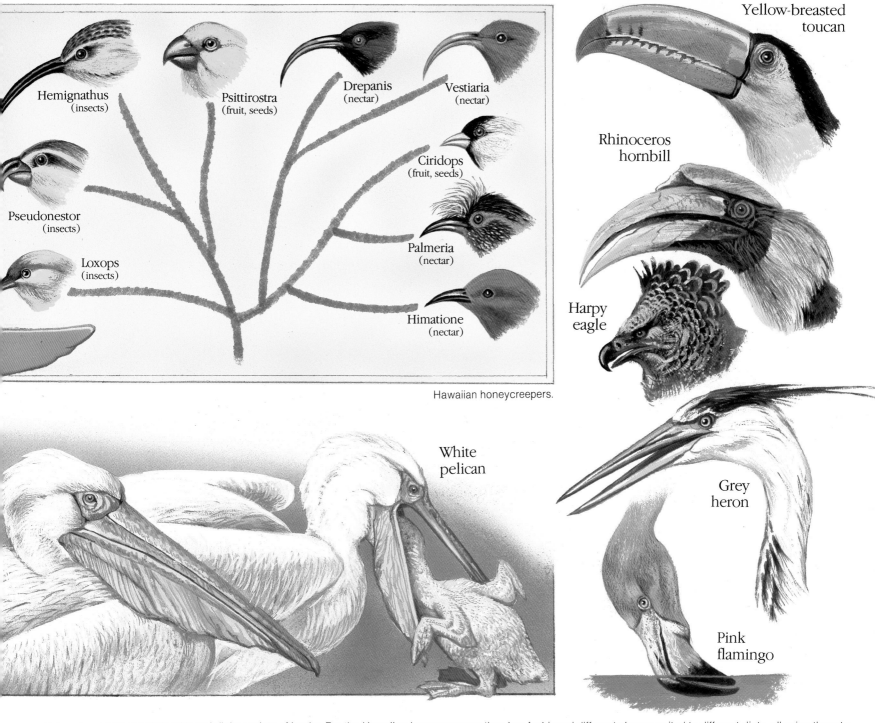

Hawaiian honeycreepers.

Yellow-breasted toucan

Rhinoceros hornbill

Harpy eagle

White pelican

Grey heron

Pink flamingo

Hemignathus (insects)

Psittirostra (fruit, seeds)

Drepanis (nectar)

Vestiaria (nectar)

Pseudonestor (insects)

Loxops (insects)

Ciridops (fruit, seeds)

Palmeria (nectar)

Himatione (nectar)

Nature has endowed birds with an infinite variety of beaks. For the Hawaiian honeycreepers time has fashioned different shapes suited to different diets, allowing them to exploit every ecological niche on the islands. The white pelican regurgitates into the large sac beneath the beak partially digested fish, which is then used to feed its young. The toucan and the hornbill have huge and awkward beaks. In birds of prey, like the harpy eagle, the strong and sharp hooked beak serves to tear the flesh of its prey. Herons have a long and pointed beak for spearing fish, while the flamingo filters water through its curved beak, in which thin plates serve to retain the food.

THE STERNUM OR BREASTBONE

ying also requires powerful muscular bands joined the wings at one end and to the breastbone at the her, or rather to a bony crest on the latter known as e keel. The breastbone may be without a keel, as in e ancient *Archaeopteryx* and in present-day running rds (e.g. the ostrich), as the keel is always sociated with the ability to fly and with the presence suitable muscle.

EVOLUTION OF THE SKELETON

e have already seen that the skeleton of the *rchaeopteryx* possessed characteristics closer to ose of reptiles than those of birds, but in less ancient ecimens, such as the *Ichthyornis*, all the main

changes had already appeared: the keeled sternum, the wing, and the legs in three segments. In living birds, the characteristics of the skeleton are uniform; only specialists are able to identify small differences, useful in drawing up a classification scheme.

FROM TEETH TO BEAK

The class started off with a mouth bristling with sharp, conical teeth typical of animals of prey, and was quickly replaced by a bony case covering the upper and lower jaws: the beak or bill. This structure is not a novelty, it appears even in reptiles such as tortoises as well as in other species now extinct, and we shall see it again in the monotremes—very primitive mammals. It is difficult to establish whether teeth or a beak is more efficient; it can only be noted that in a highly sophisticated and evolved class such as that of the

birds, the animal with a beak instead of teeth has been able to evolve with great success so as to expand throughout the world. It is characteristic of the beak that it has a wide variety of forms and dimensions adapted to the food requirements of the environment. The great English naturalist Charles R. Darwin (1809-1882), during his voyages, was able to observe different beak adaptations in the same genus of birds, according to the type of food available in the different islands. This observation, along with others of course, underlay the great scientist's first evolutionary considerations. There are a great many examples of different beaks, all well suited to specific tasks, in birds. There are also some that seem paradoxical and absurd, as in the hornbill and toucan, but perhaps we do not yet understand the reasons and functions, as in general there are no absurd and useless structures in the organization of living creatures.

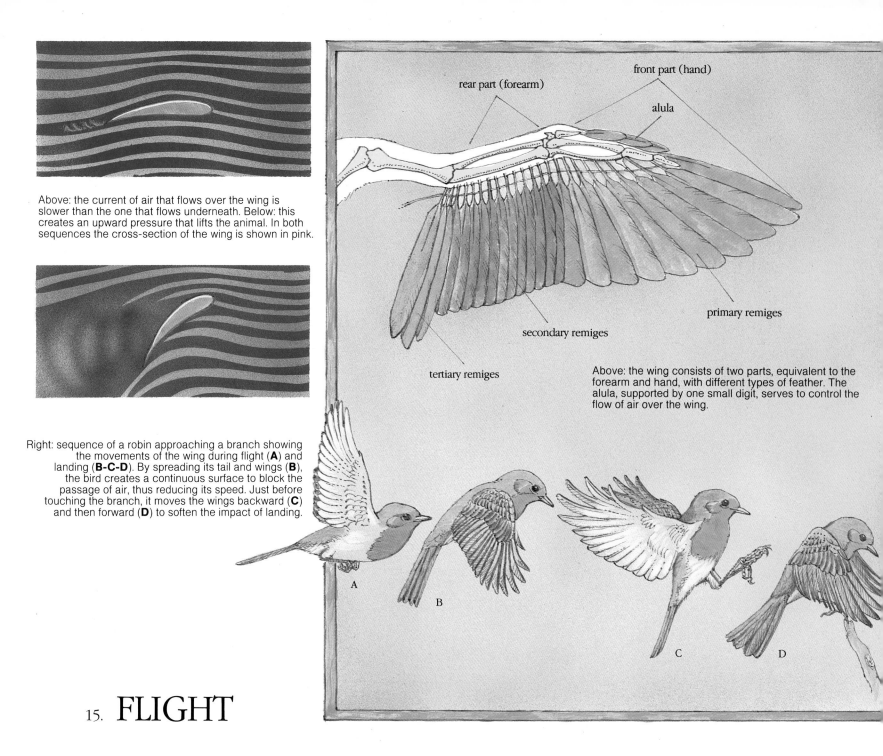

Above: the current of air that flows over the wing is slower than the one that flows underneath. Below: this creates an upward pressure that lifts the animal. In both sequences the cross-section of the wing is shown in pink.

Right: sequence of a robin approaching a branch showing the movements of the wing during flight (**A**) and landing (**B-C-D**). By spreading its tail and wings (**B**), the bird creates a continuous surface to block the passage of air, thus reducing its speed. Just before touching the branch, it moves the wings backward (**C**) and then forward (**D**) to soften the impact of landing.

rear part (forearm)

front part (hand)

alula

primary remiges

secondary remiges

tertiary remiges

Above: the wing consists of two parts, equivalent to the forearm and hand, with different types of feather. The alula, supported by one small digit, serves to control the flow of air over the wing.

A

B

C

D

15. FLIGHT

PRIMARIES AND SECONDARIES

Bird flight involves very complex mechanisms. Until fairly recently, it was thought that when the wing was lowered the bird rose and went forward: this is true, but only in part. First, two main parts can be distinguished in the wing: one of these is attached to what would be the "hand," with primary feathers, while one is connected to the forearm, with secondary feathers. The two types of feathers are easily recognizable: the primaries are characterized by a shaft (rachis) and side branches (barbs), the latter being especially developed on one side, while the secondaries have well-developed barbs on both sides.

HOW BIRDS FLY

These different forms correspond to two different functions: the rear part of the wing (or forearm), with the secondary feathers, moves comparatively little but constantly supplies supporting force, even when it

remains motionless. Let us take an airplane wing as an example: the air moves more quickly over the upper surface, thus causing the greater underwing pressure that creates the support necessary to remain suspended in the air. The analogy with the airplane wing is perfect: with movement, as a result of the force that acts under the wing, an upward thrust is created to support the airplane or the bird. Let us continue the comparison: the propeller in the airplane and the front part of the wing (or "hand") with the primary remiges in the bird perform the same function—that of providing the forward thrust. The movement of this part of the wing is highly complex; but some hypotheses have been reached on its operation through cinematography observed in slow motion. The front part of the wing moves in a semicircle: while it is moving downward it first advances and then retreats, thus generating a forward thrust as well as contributing to support. To obtain the different thrusts the feathers must not only be different, but must also project one above the other to form a continuous flat surface. When the wing rises the feathers are rotated,

thus offering only the rib to the air resistance; as soon as the wing has reached the highest point the feathers return to the original position in order to again form a continuous flat surface.

THE FEATHER: AN EXTRAORDINARY STRUCTURE

Flight is thus based on the characteristics of the feather, which constitutes one of the most extraordinary and complicated structures of all those that cover the bodies of vertebrates. Nothing in nature is at the same time so light and so strong. It is believed that the feather derives from a further specialization of the scales on reptiles. In the two structures, in fact, the first part of the development is identical, then the feather progressively acquires its particular feature: the central stem and the side barbs. From the barbs tiny branches (barbules) stick out and grip one another by means of microscopic hooks. The continuous surface obtained is at the same time extremely light and extremely strong, as it does not allow air to pass through.

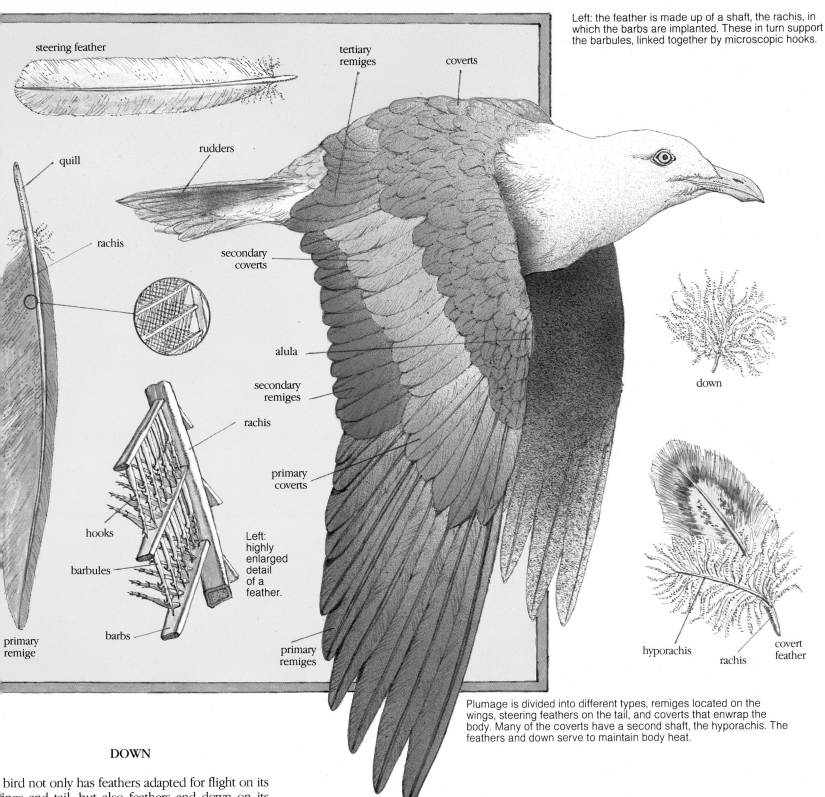

steering feather

quill

rachis

primary remige

tertiary remiges

coverts

rudders

secondary coverts

alula

secondary remiges

primary coverts

rachis

hooks

barbules

barbs

Left: highly enlarged detail of a feather.

primary remiges

Left: the feather is made up of a shaft, the rachis, in which the barbs are implanted. These in turn support the barbules, linked together by microscopic hooks.

down

hyporachis

rachis

covert feather

Plumage is divided into different types, remiges located on the wings, steering feathers on the tail, and coverts that enwrap the body. Many of the coverts have a second shaft, the hyporachis. The feathers and down serve to maintain body heat.

DOWN

bird not only has feathers adapted for flight on its ings and tail, but also feathers and down on its hole body to protect it from the cold. A bird, as we ready know, is thermoregulated at 106 °F (41 °C), a mperature that is generally higher than that of the nvironment, and hence its body tends to cool down. o limit this heat loss there are feathers called overt feathers, and under these there is down hich, by holding a layer of air, reduces the heat loss. this case, the feathers and down perform the same nctions as fur; in fact, they work better because they e able to protect even aquatic species (such as enguins), whereas fur, incapable of doing this, isappears in marine mammals such as cetaceans.

CHANGING OF FEATHERS

ven feathers grow old and wear out, so that ontinuous change is necessary. Molting generally kes place gradually, to avoid jeopardizing the efficiency of the wings. Only in certain aquatic birds (such as swans) do the wing feathers and tail feathers fall at the same time: for a while the bird is unable to fly and tries to remain hidden to avoid predators. In some species, adapted to living in environments that are periodically covered with snow, the feathers are molted twice a year in order to camouflage the color as much as possible in relation to the colors of the environment (see Chap. 17).

AN IMPORTANT GLAND

At the end of the spinal column nearly all birds have a gland (uropigea) producing a greasy secretion that the animal spreads on its feathers with its beak. This secretion has two important functions: the greasiness serves to maintain the elasticity of the feathers, which would otherwise become very brittle, and it contains a provitamin which in light is converted to the complex and important vitamin D. When we see a bird preening itself, we generally think it is cleaning itself; in reality, it is dirtying itself with its greasy glandular secretion while it is unwittingly taking its vitamin D ration and refastening the barbule hooks that have accidentally opened.

cerebellum

telencephalon

mesencephalon

Bird's brain.

Camarhynchus pallidus

A finch in the Galapagos Islands, the *Camarhynchus pallidus*, uses cactus spines to pry insect grubs out of rotten wood, thereby displaying "intelligent" behavior.

The imprinting discovered by Konrad Lorenz is typical of the behavior of many birds. The drawing shows goslings whose first sight at the moment of birth had been the great naturalist. As a result he became their "parent" despite the vast difference in appearance from the true parents.

16. INTELLIGENCE

THE CEREBELLUM

It is an ovoidal mass, rich in convolutions, occupying the central and rear part of the brain in birds. This center is entrusted with the tasks of coordinating the animal's muscular masses and its balance. The greater volume of this nerve area, as compared with reptiles, is by no means surprising, since the cerebellum must control the muscular masses of breast and legs which are far greater in birds.

THE MESENCEPHALON AND TELENCEPHALON

The doubts and uncertainties start when the other two centers are examined. The mesencephalon, which is very bulky, consists of two spherical masses located at the sides of the brain. In the lower vertebrates this area controls the animal's entire nervous system, but in mammals it is reduced when another center, the telencephalon, takes full control of the animal. In birds, on the other hand, alongside a well-developed mesencephalon, there is an even larger telencephalon consisting of two hemispheres. Both areas receive sensory impulses (acoustic, optical, etc.) and are involved in the motor responses. In birds, it is almost as if there were two brains, both capable of feeling and both capable of influencing behavior. How this can happen and what the relations are between the two centers is yet to be discovered, and it may be that this anatomical peculiarity underlies behavior which is full of inexplicable contradictions.

ARE BIRDS INTELLIGENT?

It is very difficult to define intelligence; perhaps it is closest to the truth when one considers behavior to be intelligent if it is capable of changing according to different circumstances. For example, in invertebrates, and in many vertebrates, a given stimulus always calls forth the same genetically determined response, i.e. a response caused by the characteristics of the nervous system already laid down at birth; this kind of behavior cannot be considered "intelligent," but reflexive. If the animal responds to a stimulus in a variety of ways dictated by various causes (experience, learning, etc.), it is already possible to talk about "intelligent attitudes." If birds are examined on this basis contradictory facts emerge: the *Camarhynchus pallidus*, for example, drives grubs out of rotten wood with a twig—in other words, it uses a tool with extremely complex and, hence, "intelligent" behavior. Nearly all birds can be taught something, which is a clear sign that they have the capacity to learn, and is a fundamental presupposition for intelligence. But there is no lack of contrary examples. Some birds sit lovingly on their eggs, but if an egg is moved and juts dangerously outside the nest the bird does not understand what has happened and makes no attempt to put it back in place. The cuckoo lays an egg in the nest of another species, which incubates the egg and feeds the nestling, even if it is much bigger and a different color from its own. When the young cuckoo is born, it uses its back to push the other eggs out of

the nest so that it remains the only one to be fed by the adoptive parents. This behavior seems to be intelligent, but in reality it is purely instinctive since the cuckoo continues its movement even when there are no more eggs or it is stimulated by pressure on its back. These are innate attitudes, allowing no flexibility. Nor do the adoptive parents understand that they are feeding a foreigner to the species, despite the fact that the "chick" may be three or four times as big as the mother.

IMPRINTING

This term indicates a singular nervous capacity present in many birds which was discovered and described by a great naturalist, Konrad Lorenz. When the chick breaks out of the egg the first images it gathers, the first experiences it achieves, and the first living things it sees are imprinted in its brain and will then condition all subsequent behavior. Thus, if at birth the birds see a person for a sufficiently long time, this person is looked upon as a parent and the relations with that person are typical of the newborn chicks of the species. These birds then, already at birth, have precise genetically-prepared behavior patterns, still, however, lacking the subject to which such behavior must be directed. This final consummation takes place through direct observation after birth. Even though imprinting is a fascinating and curious mode of behavior, it can certainly not be defined as intelligent.

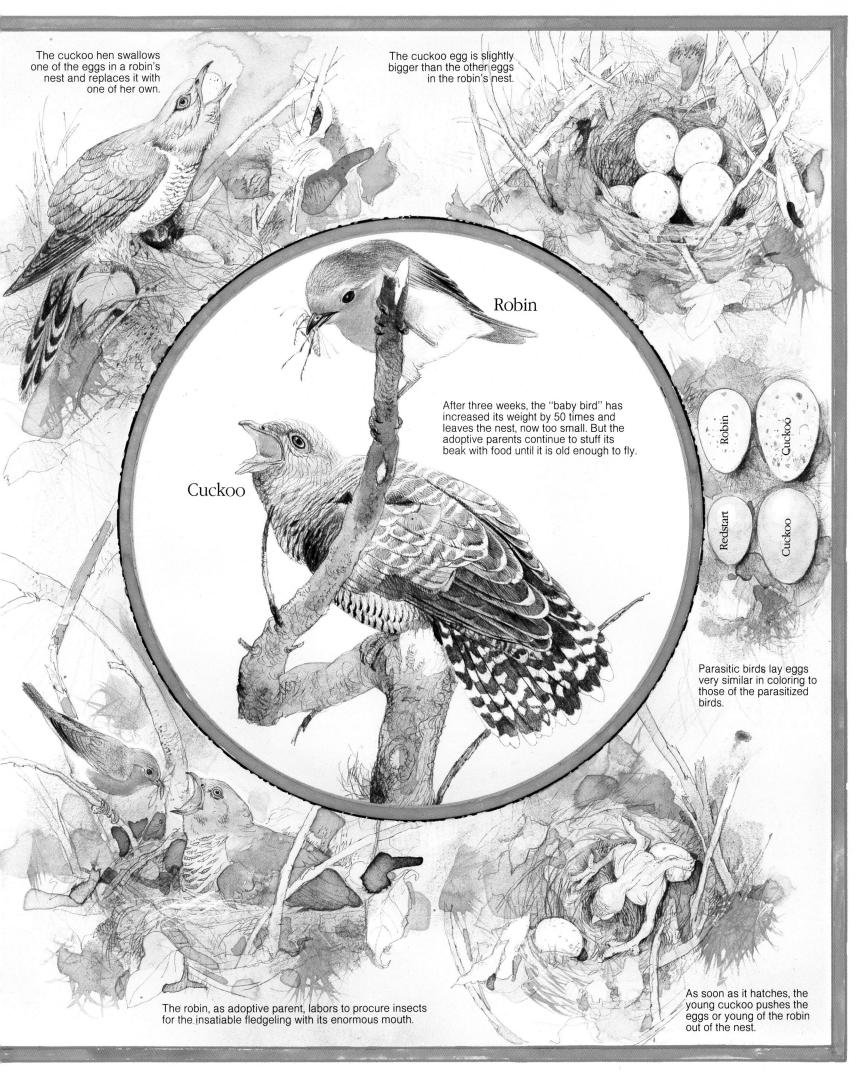

The cuckoo hen swallows one of the eggs in a robin's nest and replaces it with one of her own.

The cuckoo egg is slightly bigger than the other eggs in the robin's nest.

Robin

Cuckoo

After three weeks, the "baby bird" has increased its weight by 50 times and leaves the nest, now too small. But the adoptive parents continue to stuff its beak with food until it is old enough to fly.

Robin

Cuckoo

Redstart

Cuckoo

Parasitic birds lay eggs very similar in coloring to those of the parasitized birds.

The robin, as adoptive parent, labors to procure insects for the insatiable fledgeling with its enormous mouth.

As soon as it hatches, the young cuckoo pushes the eggs or young of the robin out of the nest.

Ptarmigan in summer

Ptarmigan in winter

In order to escape the notice of predators, the ptarmigan camouflages itself to accord with its surroundings, gradually changing its brown summer plumage into a white winter one.

17. COLOR

CAMOUFLAGE

In the majority of birds, the colors of the plumage are combined to neutralize the effect of their shadows. Thus, the darker colors are arranged on the upper parts of the body, on which the light falls more intensely, while the lighter ones are located on the underbody where they are often in the shade. This different distribution of color, already seen in fish, serves to break up the animal's outline. Naturally, there is also chromatic adaptation to the environment; in inhabitants of the forest foliage green is predominant, while those that habitually live on the ground tend toward brown. We have seen (Chap. 15) that there can also be seasonal variations: for example, the ptarmigan is brown in summer, while at the approach of winter it changes its feathers and becomes white.

OSTENTATION

Among birds, however, we also find the opposite phenomenon of ostentation. The males of some species flaunt highly colored and gaudy plumage, developed specifically to be noted. In these cases, even the form of the feathers departs from the usual scheme: thus we find barbs that are slender and spaced to resemble down.

In general, the showiness of the cock contrasts with the camouflaged livery of the hen, which has duller colors. It is a classic example of sexual dimorphism— the big difference in colors and size between male and female of the same genus—determined by the procedures with which couples are formed in the reproduction period.

MATING: COLOR AND MOVEMENTS

It is the hen that selects and accepts the cock: first, however, she must be stimulated by her suitor's appearance. Thus, with the passing generations the females, by continuing to choose the males with the most striking colors and the longest and most unusual feathers, have created increasingly showy specimens. The peacock is an example of sexual selection brought about by the females. Its marvelous tail, strewn with all the colors of the rainbow, is pompously displayed during mating. Unfortunately, the beauty of the male's plumage, together with the hen's, also attracts the attention of predatory animals.

In the mating season, nearly all the males perform "dances" or simpler figures which, together with the colors, are designed to entice the females. These movements seem strange to us only because they are performed out of their usual context and in exaggerated form, but their origin is entirely natural; for example, they repeat, in enhanced form, the movement of rising in flight or preening their feathers, or they may imitate the seeking and offering of food.

PARASITISM

Birds are often praised for their skill in making nests, the patience with which they hatch the eggs, and the care they lavish on their young. But, as always happens in every family, there is no lack of "black sheep." In Chap. 16, we saw the cuckoo hen laying her eggs in other birds' nests and then not taking care of them. An African passeriform bird, characterized by the cock's long tail, the paradise whydah, carries out a more

Cormorant

Shelduck

Mating is often preceded by a courtship ritual that imitates the bird's natural gestures in its daily life: the cormorant looks as if it is about to take off; the shelduck pretends to preen itself.

refined type of parasitism: it lays its eggs in the nest of another small passerine bird, the melba finch, which is very different in appearance. When it emerges from the egg, the little whydah is almost indistinguishable from the melba finch young. This strong resemblance persists for about five weeks, sufficient time for the nestling to become independent of the adoptive parents and to leave the nest, when the whydah acquires the typical color and features of its species.

Peacock

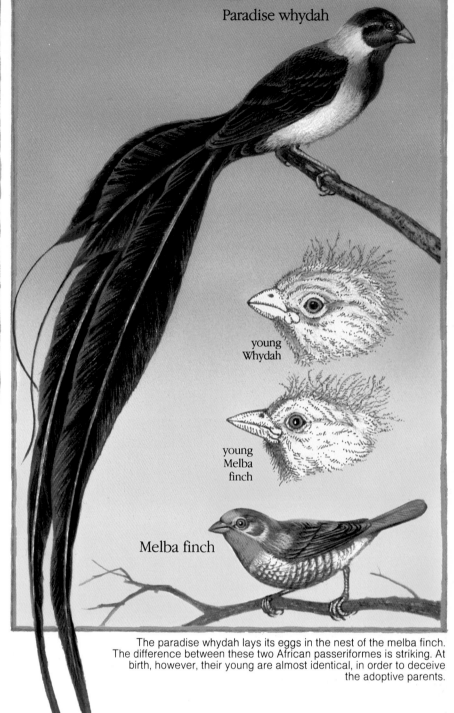

Paradise whydah

young
Whydah

young
Melba
finch

Melba finch

peacock
feather

feather
of
Pterido-
phora
alberti

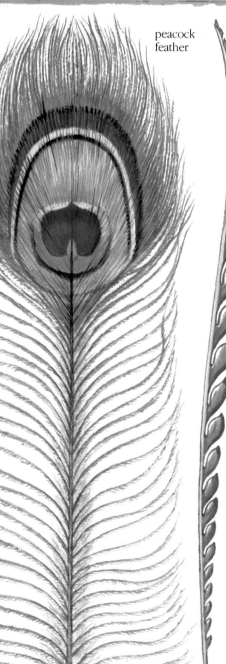

Above: the majority of birds display marked sexual dimorphism, i.e. a great difference in appearance between male and female. An obvious example is the peacock: the male (right) shows off its gaudy tail to impress the much less brightly colored female.

The paradise whydah lays its eggs in the nest of the melba finch. The difference between these two African passeriformes is striking. At birth, however, their young are almost identical, in order to deceive the adoptive parents.

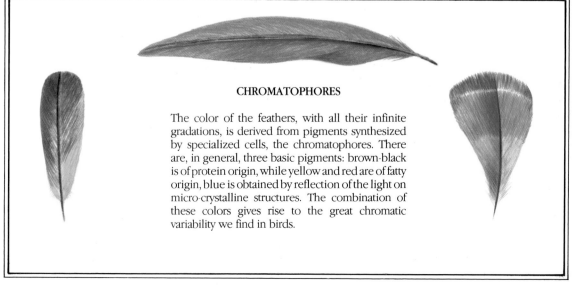

CHROMATOPHORES

The color of the feathers, with all their infinite gradations, is derived from pigments synthesized by specialized cells, the chromatophores. There are, in general, three basic pigments: brown-black is of protein origin, while yellow and red are of fatty origin, blue is obtained by reflection of the light on micro-crystalline structures. The combination of these colors gives rise to the great chromatic variability we find in birds.

Red ovenbird

The red ovenbird builds its nest out of wet clay that hardens in the sun.

The African village weaver starts by joining two branches (**1**), then forms a ring (**2**) that serves as a framework for the spherical nest (**3**). The entrance faces downward.

Village weaver

Weaverbirds build a nest out of interwoven blades of grass suspended from a bra

Australian mallee-fowl

The nest of the Australian mallee-fowl is a hole dug in the ground with a thick bed of leaves on which the eggs are laid and then covered with a layer of sand. The warmth produced by the rotting leaves incubates the eggs. If the temperature drops, the male digs up the sand, spreads it to heat up in the sun and then covers the eggs up again.

18. NEST, EGGS, PARENTAL CARE

MASONS, WEAVERS, AND GARDENERS BUILD THEIR HOMES

Even if there are idlers like the cuckoo and the whydah, birds are generally highly skilled nest-builders. The animal does not learn the trade from anyone: the procedure necessary for performing the work is already imprinted in its brain at birth. The main material with which the nest is made consists of twigs of all sizes which form the framework, while the inside is stuffed with softer materials such as old feathers, tufts of wool, slender blades of grass, etc. The instrument used is almost solely the beak; however, the bird uses its body to shape the inside of the nest. Both sexes are generally involved in this task, requiring not only skill but also a large expenditure of energy.

Some birds, commonly known as "weavers," are capable of plaiting blades of grass with great care, knotting them, and sewing together the edges of

leaves in order to form extremely complex nests. A more refined technique is the use of materials that solidify. Swallows collect wet clay in their beaks to build the nest. When the clay is dry, the walls become solid and it only remains to line the interior with soft material. Satin bower birds act in a singular way. In the mating season the cock skillfully builds a hut; then in front of the entrance he tidily spreads the most varied material, all in lively colors: pebbles, flowers, berries, and anything else showy he can find. The sole purpose of all this display of color is to attract the other sex, clearly sensitive to the call of colors. When a female finally arrives, the pair retires into the dark of the hut where mating takes place. When this is over, the cock goes away and resumes his bachelor life while the hen abandons the hut, which should perhaps be called a *garçonnière*, and builds a sounder, more efficient nest.

FORMATION OF THE EGG

The egg is made by the hen in accordance with technique reminiscent of an assembly line. A bird egg, very similar to a reptile's egg (see the volum *Reptiles*, Chap. 2), must have a large reserve of foo substances, water, and a shell sufficiently strong support the animal's weight during incubation. Fro the ovary, a small red sphere is detached, this is t yolk which contains the embryo which will becom the new bird and a large quantity of nutriti substances. As it descends along the oviduct, the yo receives the chalaza which holds it in position in t center of the egg, then the protein and water ri albumen, then a slender membrane, and finally t shell. Inside the egg the new bird grows and feeds, a only when development is complete can it fina emerge into the open.

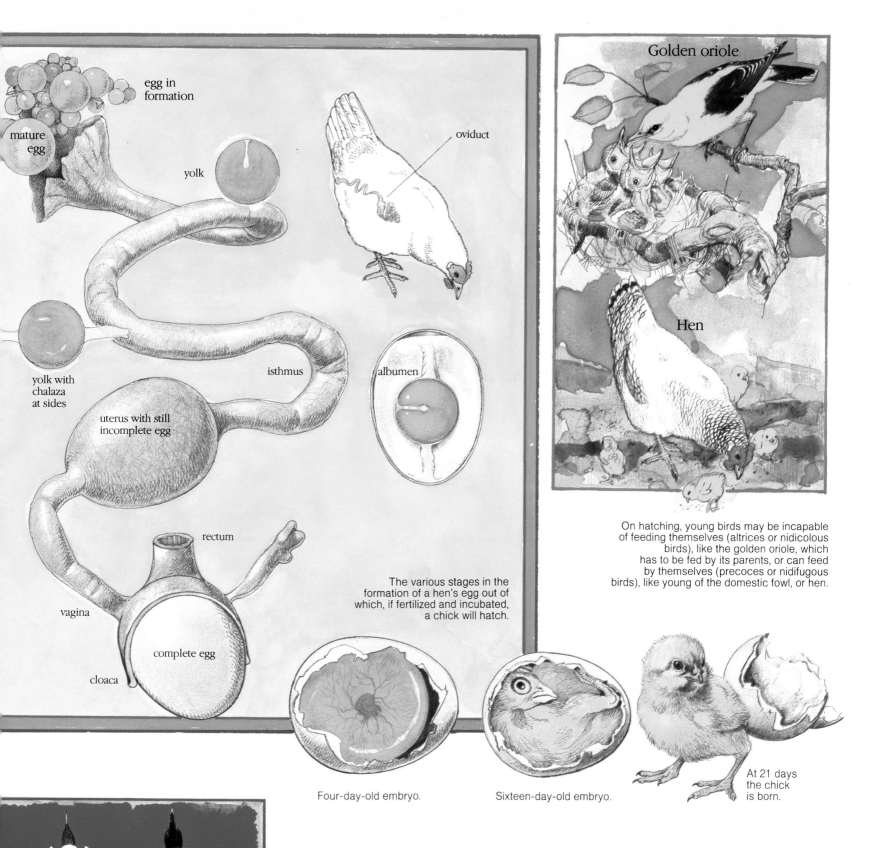

egg in formation

mature egg

yolk

oviduct

yolk with chalaza at sides

isthmus

albumen

uterus with still incomplete egg

rectum

vagina

complete egg

cloaca

The various stages in the formation of a hen's egg out of which, if fertilized and incubated, a chick will hatch.

Golden oriole

Hen

On hatching, young birds may be incapable of feeding themselves (altrices or nidicolous birds), like the golden oriole, which has to be fed by its parents, or can feed by themselves (precoces or nidifugous birds), like young of the domestic fowl, or hen.

Four-day-old embryo.

 Sixteen-day-old embryo.

At 21 days the chick is born.

Gull   Guillemot

Many birds have areas rich in blood vessels, and therefore warmer, on their underbellies. These are known as incubating plates and their number varies according to species.

INCUBATION

For development of the embryo inside the egg, it is absolutely essential that the egg should be kept warm. The internal part of the nest stuffed with soft materials may be a help, but it is normally the parents that supply the necessary heat. In fact, the warmth does not derive so much from the animal's own heat as from areas of skin located on its underbody—the so-called "incubating plates"—which, being very rich in blood, are very warm. The task of sitting on the eggs may be carried out alternately by both sexes or the hen may never leave the nest, in which case the cock feeds her. The emperor penguin, which lives in frozen lands, keeps the egg between its feet and warms it with a fold of its skin.

CARE OF THE YOUNG

At birth, birds behave in one of two distinct ways: either the unfledged nestling is absolutely incapable of providing for its own food needs, or it is capable of seeking its own nourishment. The case of farmyard hens is known to everyone: as soon as it comes out of the egg the chick is able to walk and peck. In the case of "nidicolous" young, either both parents, or one of them, feed the constantly hungry nestlings, always with their mouths open. This function is a purely reflex action; anything having the form and color of an open mouth induces the adult birds to bring it food. The story is told of a bird which, having nested close to the bank of a pool, fed wily carp that had learned to open their mouths at the bird's arrival.

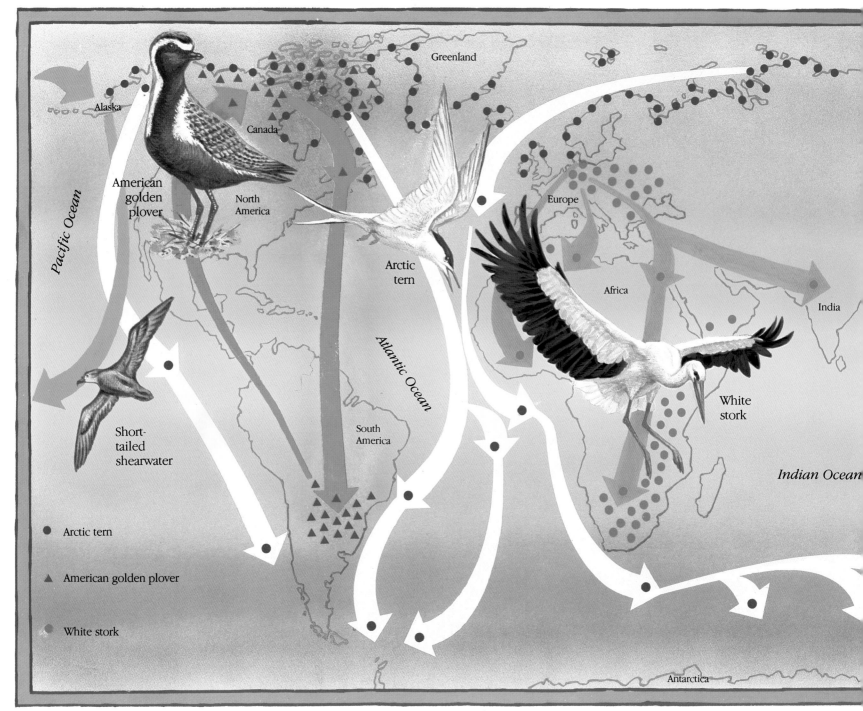

Greenland

Alaska

Canada

North America

Pacific Ocean

American golden plover

Arctic tern

Atlantic Ocean

Europe

Africa

India

Short-tailed shearwater

South America

White stork

Indian Ocean

● Arctic tern

▲ American golden plover

● White stork

Antarctica

19. MIGRATIONS

WHY DO BIRDS MIGRATE?

What is it that induces birds to migrate, and how did this phenomenon originate? We have no direct evidence and must resort to suppositions. If we observe the ring ouzel, which lives in the mountains and does not make migrations, we find that at the arrival of winter it moves down to the plain, returning to its usual territories in spring. This simple behavior may lie at the origin of migrations—at first short, then increasingly long distances—during which the birds learn to find their way back to their places of origin. Another example is that of insect-eating birds, which spread from the tropical forests rich in insects to other latitudes in search of food, returning to the starting-point when winter sets in and the insects disappear. Perhaps the big periodical glaciations that have followed one another on Earth during the last million years have caused imposing movements of animals— including birds—in one direction, with inverse movements during the interglacial ages.

It is easier to say what physiologically induces birds to migrate. After the reproductive period the animal's endocrine glands undergo drastic regression; they change feathers and accumulate fat under the epidermis, especially in species that do not feed during the journey. These physiological preparations are ordered by a gland at the base of the brain—the pituitary gland—which regulates nearly all activities of the organism. The switch that prepares for migration is probably triggered by photoperiodism, i.e. the differing lengths of day and night.

orientation turns

sundial magnetic compass

600 mi. (1,000 km)

To find its way home the pigeon makes use of different senses and methods according to the distance involved.

Arctic Ocean

Alaska

Pacific Ocean

Short-tailed shearwater

Australia

Tasmania

olfactory sensations	sight	dovecot
60 mi. (100 km)	6 mi. (10 km)	

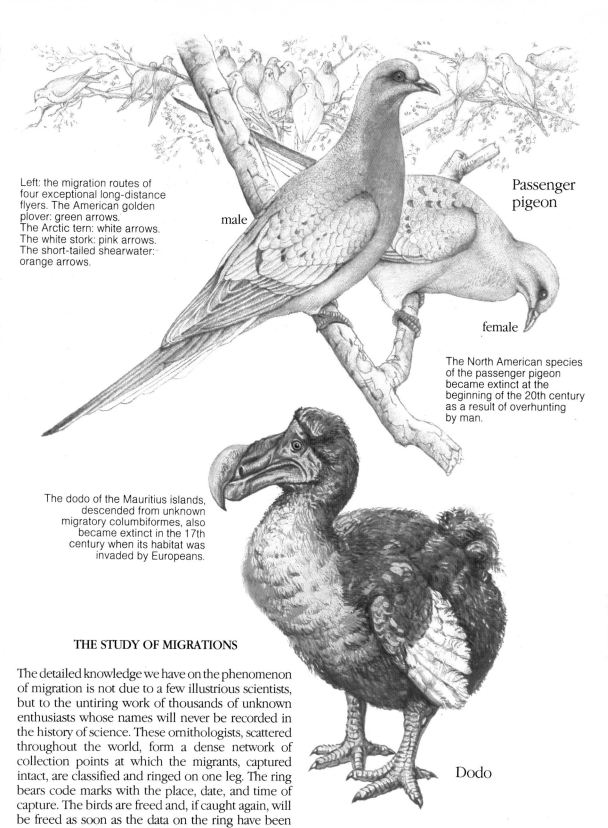

Left: the migration routes of four exceptional long-distance flyers. The American golden plover: green arrows. The Arctic tern: white arrows. The white stork: pink arrows. The short-tailed shearwater: orange arrows.

male

Passenger pigeon

female

The North American species of the passenger pigeon became extinct at the beginning of the 20th century as a result of overhunting by man.

The dodo of the Mauritius islands, descended from unknown migratory columbiformes, also became extinct in the 17th century when its habitat was invaded by Europeans.

Dodo

THE STUDY OF MIGRATIONS

The detailed knowledge we have on the phenomenon of migration is not due to a few illustrious scientists, but to the untiring work of thousands of unknown enthusiasts whose names will never be recorded in the history of science. These ornithologists, scattered throughout the world, form a dense network of collection points at which the migrants, captured intact, are classified and ringed on one leg. The ring bears code marks with the place, date, and time of capture. The birds are freed and, if caught again, will be freed as soon as the data on the ring have been recorded. All data converge on the collection centers, where the migratory route can be established.

WHAT GUIDES THEM?

A special field of research establishes what guides birds to their destination so that they do not get lost. Birds have different methods of finding the way. Some of them move by day and base their direction on the position of the Sun or, if there is none, on the polarized light emitted by its rays. The stars guide migrants that fly by night. This surprising discovery emerged from studies made in a planetarium. Recently, it was demonstrated that some birds are able to perceive the lines of the Earth's magnetic field. We know that the compass always indicates the north because its magnetized needle orients itself along the magnetic lines of the Earth. It now seems that these birds have a kind of internal compass—due to the presence in their bodies, it is not known exactly where, of microscopic magnetite crystals—which guides them during migration.

RETURN TO THE NEST

For thousands of years, man has known the extraordinary capacity of homing pigeons to return to their nests, and in the past he has exploited it widely. Today, the pigeon is used above all for study, to understand what signals always take it home, and it has been found that it uses various aids. From 600 to 60 miles (1,000 to 100 kilometers), it is guided by its internal compass and the Sun; from 60 to 6 miles (100 to 10 km), the sense of smell acts—or in other words the odor of its territory shows it the right way; at less than 6 miles (10 km), it recognizes the features of its environment by sight and finally reaches the nest.

20. EXTINCT RUNNING BIRDS

Sixty-five million years ago, as we already know, the dinosaurs and other reptiles that had been dominant throughout the Secondary Era, disappeared from the earth. For some, the hecatomb occurred within the space of a few years, while for others it took nearly a million. From that fateful date, various areas of the Earth were free of dominant forms and, hence, open for settlement by other animals without striking a blow. During this period the birds were in full expansion, whereas mammals were still represented by small and unspecialized animals.

THE BRIEF REIGN OF THE RUNNING BIRDS

The first to dash for possession of the zones left free by the reptiles were the birds that rejected flight and sought to establish themselves permanently in all territories. There was a moment in history, between 55 and 65 million years ago, in which the dominant vertebrates on earth were non-flying birds. But their sway did not last long: the unexpected evolution of mammals, with the appearance of a number of orders we now know, led to the progressive establishment of our class and the steady disappearance of the great running birds. Some disappeared from the scene as much as 20-30 million years ago, while others which had succeeded in coming down to us were exterminated by man. Today, however, some birds strictly linked to life on the ground survive on different continents, albeit with difficulty.

DIATRYMA

This powerful bird, which had a beak 16 inches (40 centimeters) long, and two strong hind legs armed with large claws, was dominant 50 million years ago in North America and Europe. It was perhaps the largest animal on earth at that period, so it must have had no dangerous enemies and could therefore develop gigantism. From the characteristics of the skull, this ancient giant seems to be related to the elegant crested seriema or crested screamer living in Brazil.

PHORORHACOS

This giant may also be related to the seriema, even if the external appearance is completely different. The *Phororhacos inflatus*, up to 5 feet (1.5 meters) tall, lived in South America from 20 to 40 million years ago and constituted a dangerous bird of prey. The great beak with the typical shape of the hunter and the legs with toes armed with strong claws indicate an exceptional capacity for preying and tearing the victim to pieces. The *Phororhacos* was unable to fly, but still had wings, albeit reduced to stumps useful perhaps only for balancing its body when running.

The reign of these giants may have ended with the appearance of the medium- and large-sized carnivores that inserted themselves firmly in the ecological niche reserved to beasts of prey.

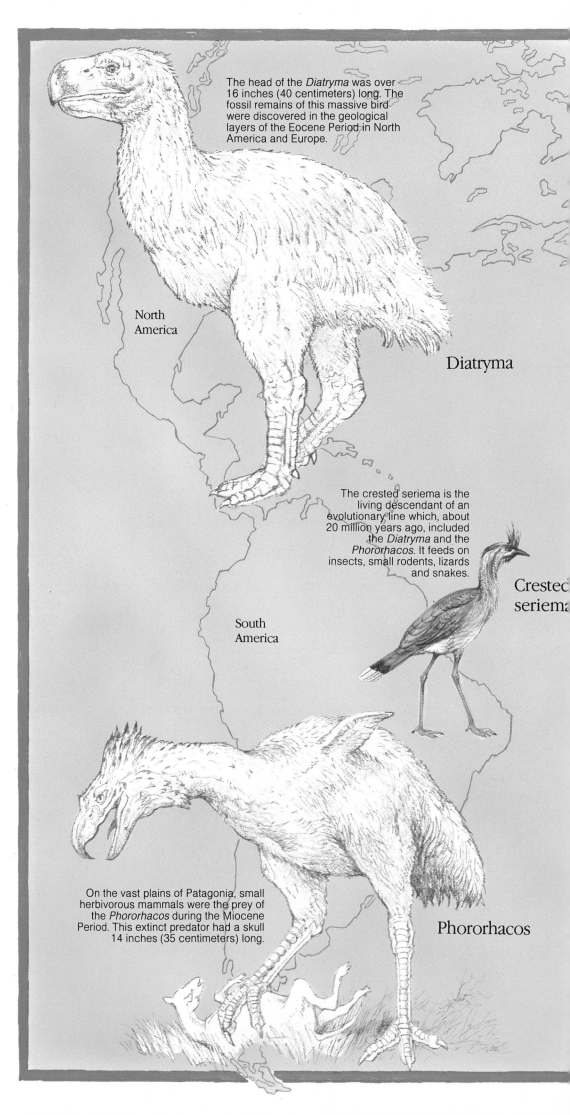

The head of the *Diatryma* was over 16 inches (40 centimeters) long. The fossil remains of this massive bird were discovered in the geological layers of the Eocene Period in North America and Europe.

North America

Diatryma

The crested seriema is the living descendant of an evolutionary line which, about 20 million years ago, included the *Diatryma* and the *Phororhacos*. It feeds on insects, small rodents, lizards and snakes.

South America

Crested seriema

On the vast plains of Patagonia, small herbivorous mammals were the prey of the *Phororhacos* during the Miocene Period. This extinct predator had a skull 14 inches (35 centimeters) long.

Phororhacos

Aepyornis

Dinornis

In Madagascar floods sometimes bring to light enormous fossil eggs of *Aepyornis maximus*, the extinct bird reconstructed above.

The gigantic *Dinornis*, now extinct, consumed a large quantity of vegetable food in order to maintain their enormous bulk. In the remains of their stomachs many pebbles have also been found, which they swallowed to grind their food better.

Here are two giant birds in comparison with man. While the *Dinornis* was taller, 11.5 feet (3.5 meters), the *Aepyornis* was heavier, up to 970 pounds (440 kilos).

Aepyornis

Dinornis

Man

DINORNIS

In New Zealand, where the placental mammals with their large carnivores had not arrived, there lived what was perhaps the biggest bird that has ever existed, the *Dinornis maximus*, up to 15 feet (4.5 meters) tall. This giant had strong, sturdy legs like those of an elephant, but furnished with robust toes. From the characteristics of the beak, it must be presumed that the animal had feeding habits similar to those of the present-day ostrich; hence, it would not have disdained small prey, but its favorite diet must have been vegetarian. The eggs were also enormous, over 12 inches (30 centimeters) long.

This non-flying bird managed to coexist with man until the appearance of the colonizers with their guns; seeing a precious source of food in the huge animal, they unwittingly decreed its end. The last gunshot aimed at a *Dinornis*, which the native Maoris called

Moa, was fired in 1770, since which time only a lot of bones, some eggs, and some rare feathers have survived of this stupendous animal. The one we see on this page is only a reconstruction based on skeletal remains.

AEPYORNIS

In Africa, during the Tertiary Era, and also in Madagascar in times closer to us, another giant over 6.5 feet (2 meters) tall lived—the *Aepyornis maximus*. This bird was probably dominant on the African continent before the arrival of the great carnivores, by which it was slaughtered. In Madagascar, on the other hand, protected by the stretch of sea separating the island from Africa, the bird succeeded in coming down to us only to perish ignobly before the power of hunters in 1650.

21. LIVING RUNNING BIRDS
(Ratitae)

The living ratite or cursorial or running birds include the most primitive birds in existence (paleognaths), all characterized by the inability to fly—with the consequent greater or lesser reduction of the forelimb. Although distributed on nearly all the continents, they are continuously decreasing in numbers and some species even risk extinction.

TINAMIFORMES

In appearance they look like partridges or quails, the size of a hen; they have wings and strong muscles for flying, but their skeletal characteristics show that they belong to the running birds. Many paleontologists consider this order to be almost at the origin of all

on this sense to solve the problem of finding food. It lives in the forests of New Zealand and may be related to the huge *Dinornis.* Its smallness, about the size of a hen, and its timid, fearful character have protected it from the destruction wreaked by colonizers; but the introduction of dogs and cats that have run wild into its habitat has quickly reduced its numbers. Today strict protectionist measures seem to have stopped the danger of its extinction.

CASUARIIFORMES

These are the great runners of Australia: the emu, the most typical representative, reaches nearly 6.5 feet (2 meters) in height. Their bodies are covered with

broad expanses of the South American pampas. It i[s] very fast runner, capable even of competi[ng] victoriously with the horse. The rhea's flesh [is] appreciated, whereas the feathers are of no value. T[he] rheas, although decreasing in number, do not r[un] any danger of extinction.

STRUTHIONIFORMES

The ostrich with its height of 8 feet (2.5 meters) is t[he] largest living bird. The area over which ostriches we[re] spread was very large, including not only Africa, b[ut] also southern Europe and Asia as far as the desert [of] Mongolia. Today it lives only in limited territories [of] Africa. The ostrich's typical environment is the bro[ad]

Left: the gauchos of the pampas hunt the fleet-footed rhea, pursuing it on horseback and catching it with the "bolas," which twist round the bird's legs.

Common rhea

North America

South America

Distribution of running birds. Rheiformes: dark green. Tinamiformes: light green. Ostriches: pink. Cassowaries: violet. Emus: red. Kiwis: light blue.

birds, and certainly the first step in rejection of flight. Tinamous, found in Central and South America (for example the crested tinamou), prefer to hop along the ground, only when frightened do they make a short and clumsy flight that sometimes ends with indecorous falls.

APTERYGIFORMES

The name means "birds without wings," although in reality there are wings, but reduced to featherless stumps. The most typical representative is the kiwi, whose name recalls its nocturnal cry. It is not seen during the day, as it remains hidden in the depths of the undergrowth; it emerges only at night to start hunting for insects or worms, which it unearths through its refined sense of smell, the only bird to rely

downy feathers, also found on their small wings. They are excellent runners and touch speeds of about 30 miles (50 kilometers) an hour. Some cassowaries have a helmet-like bony excrescence on the head, perhaps as a protection for the skull in case of any collisions with natural obstacles while running. At one time, they were numerous and could be seen in great flocks at the drinking-place. Today, after the usual slaughter by the white man for pure amusement, they are greatly reduced in numbers and do not let anyone approach them.

RHEIFORMES

The common rhea, or American ostrich, is thus named because it greatly resembles the well-known African runner, even though it is smaller. It lives only in the

Crested tinamou

The male incubates and guards the eggs laid by the female in a nest set in the grass.

Ostrich

female

male

On the savannas where they live, ostriches find fruit and seeds, leaves and shoots; they also eat insects and lizards.

expanse of the savanna with high grass and occasional groups of trees. It is by no means rare to see herds of herbivores (zebras, giraffes, gnus) grazing together with ostriches. These birds have survived being hunted by the great beasts of prey through senses always on the alert, and their sturdy beaks and powerful legs furnished with large claws. Ostriches have the reputation for being fearful to the point of hiding their head in the sand at the smallest alarm; this belief is absolutely false. But it is true that the animal swallows any object, whether wood, metal, plastic or anything else. During the last century, ostriches ran the risk of extinction owing to the then current fashion of using their feathers. The very high price they reached led to ruthless hunting of these birds, attenuated only by the introduction of breeding-farms. Then, the fashion changed and the birds began once again to wander undisturbed on the savannas. Today, the ostriches run no specific risk, except for the progressive reduction of their territories.

Asia

Africa

New Guinea

Australia

New Zealand

There are three distinct species of cassowary, differing in size and in crest. This is the double-wattled cassowary.

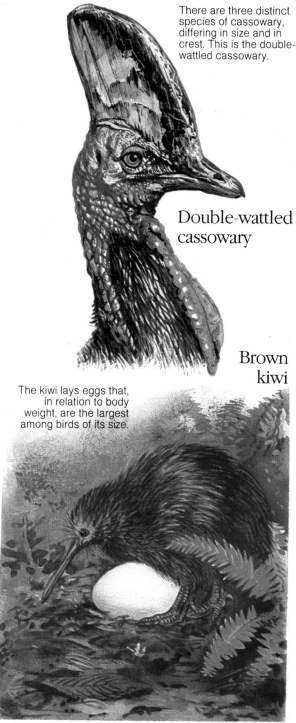

Double-wattled cassowary

Brown kiwi

Emu

An emu leading its young to a water hole on the arid plains of Australia. In this species, too, it is the male that incubates and rears the brood, which may contain as many as eight chicks.

The kiwi lays eggs that, in relation to body weight, are the largest among birds of its size.

Emperor penguin

The emperor penguin lives on the ice sheets of Antarctica; it holds the chick between its legs, keeping it warm with the abdomen. It incubates the single egg in the same way.

King penguin

The king penguin, here seen hunting fish underwater, is distinguished from the emperor by its smaller size and a different patch on the neck.

22. PENGUINS AND AUKS
(Spbenisciformes and Charadriiformes)

The origin of these singular swimming birds, the penguins, inhabitants of the southern hemisphere only, is very ancient; they were in fact present on the Earth about 50 million years ago, when modern birds had yet to appear or were at the start of their evolution.

HOW THEY SWIM

The structure of the skeleton is much changed in comparison with the general scheme of birds. The forelimbs are converted to large sturdy fins supplying the thrust for swimming. The hind limbs are used in the water as directional rudders, thus losing much of their mobility. This adaptation makes the penguin a good and very fast swimmer, capable of chasing and catching any fish, or through quick and repeated changes of direction escaping the many enemies that threaten its underwater life. Killer whales, dolphins,

sharks, and seals hunt penguins, especially when they are gathered in great flocks during the reproduction period.

HOW THEY WALK

The skill in swimming is offset by extreme clumsiness when the penguin moves on land. With the hind limbs pushed back and almost rigid it is unable to walk, at most it can hop, often with the feet together. It is always a comical sight to see penguins move on land or on ice, but this serious drawback does not expose them to dangers, since out of the water they have no enemies.

THE COLD

The penguin has to defend itself against the intense cold of the South Pole waters, and the even lower air

temperatures. The feathers have changed grea becoming squatter and shorter, more like scales, a projecting one above the other to form a continuc sheath that traps a layer of air and insulates the s underneath. This system of protection from the cc works much better than the fur of mammals, which ineffectual in icy water, to the extent that whales not have any. Whales and penguins, however, hav layer of fat under the skin which further insulates muscles and the viscera below.

REPRODUCTION

Penguins, like all birds, lay and hatch eggs, and in reproduction season they come out of the water perform the nuptial ceremony. On this occasion, shores of the continents and islands they frequent animated with thousands of birds intent on lay eggs and sitting on them. The emperor penguin,

Great auk

Today the great auk can only be found, embalmed, in museums. It died out last century owing to man's ruthless hunting.

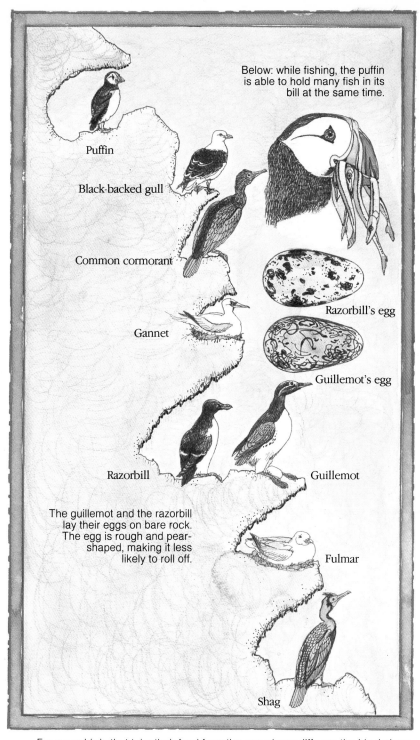

Below: while fishing, the puffin is able to hold many fish in its bill at the same time.

Puffin

Black-backed gull

Common cormorant

Gannet

Razorbill's egg

Guillemot's egg

Razorbill

Guillemot

The guillemot and the razorbill lay their eggs on bare rock. The egg is rough and pear-shaped, making it less likely to roll off.

Fulmar

Shag

For many birds that take their food from the sea, sheer cliffs are the ideal place to lay eggs and live out of danger from mammalian predators. Some birds of prey, like the great black-backed gull, make their way into these communities in order to steal eggs and young.

the largest, prefers to lay on the bare sheets of pack . It makes no nest and, in order to prevent the gle egg from freezing, keeps the egg between its t, warming it in the folds of skin. Development is w, and the chick is dependent on the parents for eks or months. This is a critical period: many birds, pecially gulls, are particularly fond of penguin eggs d may even attack the newborn young. Only when y have reached, or actually surpassed, the size of parents do the offspring venture into the sea to d their own food.

THE "PENGUINS" OF THE NORTHERN HEMISPHERE: ALCIDS

the north of the equator, in the arctic zones, there no penguins, but there are similar birds, cupying the same ecological niche—the alcids.

Like the penguins, these animals are adapted for swimming and move awkwardly on land. Unlike their distant relations of the South Pole, however, the alcids can also fly, and some of them make long journeys to reach their areas of reproduction. The zones favored by the alcids are chiefly concentrated in the Bering Sea and on the cliffs washed by the Arctic Ocean.

THE GREAT AUK

Now extinct, it was the only alcid unable to fly; its wings had lost their long feathers and resembled the penguins' flippers. Its carriage was erect and its movement was similar to that of the penguins, but, unfortunately for the great auk, it was a bird absolutely devoid of fear. In the reproduction period these birds could be found in flocks hundreds strong, intent on caring for their eggs and young, and the sailors of the

North Atlantic did not fail to land on those shores in order to obtain supplies of fresh meat with the greatest ease. When, in the nineteenth century, navigation became more intense, the great auks began to dwindle; at that time, there were no protectionist associations and hunting continued undisturbed until the last great auk was killed in 1844. Today, about a hundred embalmed specimens of this strange bird can be found in museums.

Condor

Found throughout the Andes, the condor often frequents the seashore as well, where it feeds on dead and rotting whales, seals and fish.

Lappet-faced vulture

White-headed vulture

Griffon vulture

Egyptian vultures are "intelligent" birds that, being unable to break ostrich eggs with their beaks, drop stones onto them from above.

Egyptian vulture

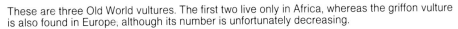

These are three Old World vultures. The first two live only in Africa, whereas the griffon vulture is also found in Europe; although its number is unfortunately decreasing.

Below: the secretary-bird feeds on snakes, rodents and insects. It is the most beautiful of the falconiformes.

23.
VULTURES, EAGLES, AND FALCONS
(Falconiformes)

Secretary-bird

This order includes birds of prey with daylight habits. Among common characteristics are the sturdy, hooked beak and the strong legs with one toe opposite the others, thus providing a firmer grip. Like the nocturnal birds of prey (Chap. 24), they are skilled hunters and seize their prey with their claws and then tear it with their beak.

VULTURES

In form and size the American vultures are very similar to the vultures of the Old Continent; but it is a classic case of convergency brought about by the same habits of life, as the two families are distantly related. The condor, the most typical representative, with a wing-span of 10 feet (3 meters), is the largest of the flying birds. It feeds on dead animals, preferably already putrefying; the beak is in fact too weak to tear off shreds of fresh meat, and hence it does not attack live animals. To identify food with its exceptionally acute sight the condor hovers at a height of hundreds of feet, then dives straight down onto any carrion. The movement does not escape its companions, even if very distant, and a large number rush to share in the

lden eagle

banquet. In Europe, Asia, and Africa we find vultures that occupy the same ecological niche as the condors, with similar form and habits. They have "more noble" origins, however, as they are related to the powerful eagle. The way in which they seek their food is similar to that of the condors, even though, having stronger claws and beak, they do not disdain small living prey.

FALCONS

This heterogeneous group includes birds, like the peregrine falcon, highly skilled in seizing their prey even during flight: they can hunt to order and return to their trainer. Falconry is a very ancient art, there are treatises in Latin and Arabic. Today it is still practiced in England and Spain.

THE SECRETARY-BIRD OR SERPENT-EATER

Its first name derives from the crest likened to a pen stuck over a writer's ear, while the alternative name refers to its favorite prey—serpents. Its hunting technique is entirely directed toward confusing the snake and tiring it out; the bird pursues it on the ground, simulating attacks and flapping its wings frantically in order to induce the reptile to strike. The secretary-bird is not immune to poisons, but endeavors to get itself bitten only on the wing feathers; when the reptile is tired, it is seized with the claws and torn with the beak.

Peregrine falcon

Mallard

THE EAGLE

Above: the peregrine falcon, a specialist in catching its prey on the wing, swoops on it at a speed of about 190 miles (300 kilometers) per hour. This bird of prey is highly esteemed in falconry.

Top: the golden eagle lays two eggs, and the young are reared by both parents. They learn to fly when two months old.

This majestic bird lives in Europe, Asia, North Africa, and North America. Indeed, in the United States it has become the very symbol of the nation. The eagle is a long-lived bird; the couples generally nest on tall trees or precipitous and inaccessible rocks. It is an excellent hunter: after discerning the prey from above through its highly acute powers of sight, the eagle captures it by attacking it with a skimming movement. It defends the nest courageously, flinging itself even on man, if necessary. The golden eagle is now unfortunately on the way to extinction.

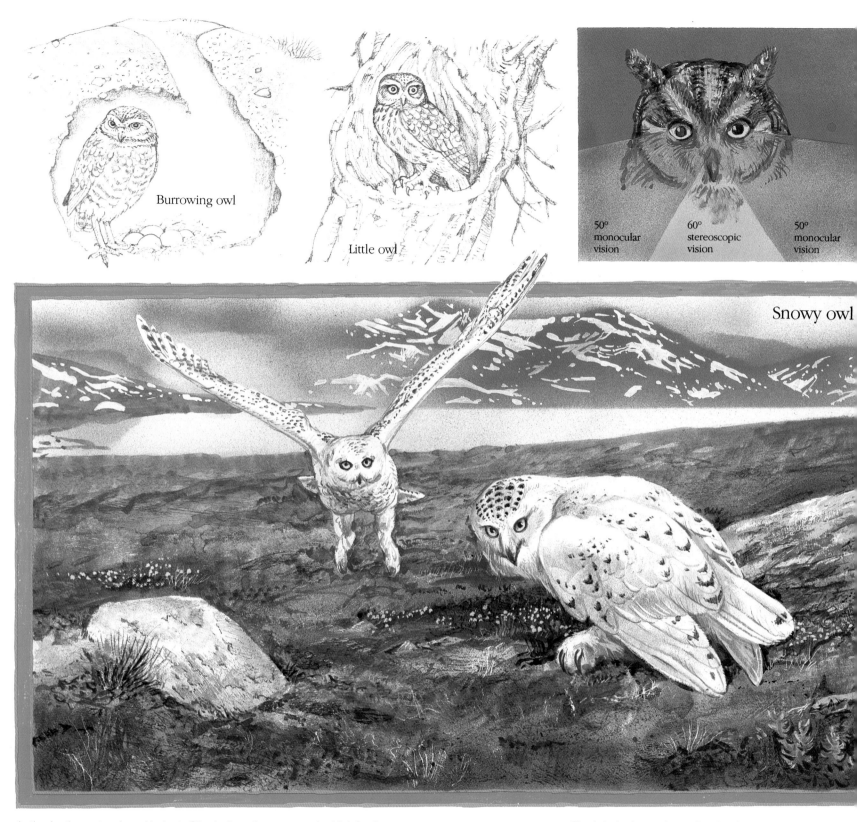

Burrowing owl

Little owl

Snowy owl

50° monocular vision | 60° stereoscopic vision | 50° monocular vision

In the Arctic wastes, from Alaska to Siberia, lives the snowy owl, which feeds on lemmings. It is distinguished by the white color of its plumage.

Top left: the burrowing owl makes its nest in the ground, wh[...] little owl lays its eggs in holes in old tree-trunks and [...]

24. NOCTURNAL BIRDS OF PREY
(Strigiformes)

This order of extant birds covers the forms that have adapted themselves to hunting in the dark of night. Common characteristics of the strigiformes are the large head, the short, squat neck, the big eyes, and the dense covering of feathers, which are so soft and light they make flight absolutely silent. Strigiformes are scattered throughout the world and adapted to any climate.

THE EYE: AN EXTRAORDINARY SENSE ORGAN

Birds in general have acute vision, but the strigiformes beat almost any other specimen of the class for efficiency. Their exceptional sight is based on a number of special features: 1) both eyes, placed on the frontal plane, focus on the prey making evaluation of the depth of field more accurate; 2) the crystalline

lens is a long way from the retina, and hence t[...] image of the prey is as though enlarged and perfec[...] focused by the pecten; 3) the visual cells are ve[...] numerous: in man they are about 2,000 per 0.[...] square lines (1 square millimeter), in strigiformes [...] to 10,000, making their visual acuity five times grea[...] than ours; 4) the pupil of their large eye can dila[...] considerably to capture the smallest ray of light. In t[...]

striated ciliary muscle

conjunctiva

cornea

crystalline lens

iris

bony ring to
reinforce the sclera

choroid

sclera

retina

pecten

optic nerve

Section
through
the eye
of an
owl.

Long-
eared
owl

The fringed edges
of their feathers
permit nocturnal
birds of prey to fly in
silence.

Found throughout Eurasia, North Africa and North America, the long-eared
owl, like all the strigiformes, has a visual field of 160°, with stereoscopic
vision at the center allowing the animal to focus on objects.

Sequence depicting a barn
owl, whose highly sensitive
hearing allows it to locate
and seize its prey in the dark.

Barn owl

tina the quantity of rhodopsin, the substance that
onverts the luminous impulse to a nervous stimulus,
high and increases the sensitivity of the eye.
through these devices the strigiformes are able to
scern and capture prey even in the feeble light of
ght.

LITTLE OWLS

enerally, the little owl is associated with witchcraft
d the evil eye, perhaps because in the silence of the
ght its cry seems like a mournful lament. A skillful
nter, it discovers prey not only with the large eyes,

but also by means of the extremely sensitive ears. The
strange form of the large, flat head seems to be a
device to channel sounds to the ear more efficiently.
Likewise, flight, which is absolutely silent, facilitates
the task of the ear as well as not betraying the
imminence of any attack. The prey, generally a rodent,
is dragged to the nest or a quiet spot, and is swallowed
whole.

THE LONG-EARED OWL

Unlike the little owl, the long-eared owl has always
enjoyed an excellent reputation and is often taken as a
symbol of wisdom, of the old sage who listens,

watches, and keeps his own counsel. Long-eared
owls, more retiring than little owls, do not generally
nest near houses, but prefer the depths of the woods
near their hunting grounds, and they explore only at
night. All strigiformes, having two eyes located on the
frontal plane, have a more restricted visual field than
birds with eyes located laterally, therefore they must
turn their whole head to look around: long-eared
owls, in particular, can turn their head 180 degrees,
and are able to explore the visual field behind them
without turning their body. The long-eared owl has
no natural enemies, only humans who, despite the
ban, continue to hunt it.

25. HUMMINGBIRDS AND QUETZALS
(Apodiformes and Trogoniformes)

Quetzal

The fabulous quetzal is one of the rarest and most beautiful birds in the world. The elegant tail, resembling a royal train, distinguishes the male, along with its splendid iridescent plumage, bright green on the back and ruby-red on the abdomen. Quetzalcoatl, the Aztec Plumed Serpent, god of the sun and the sky, in fact takes his name from the quetzal bird and *coatl*, which means serpent.

Facing page: on the American continent there are about 320 different species of hummingbird, varying in length from a maximum of 8 inches (20 centimeters) for the *Patagona gigas*, which lives in the Andes, to the bee hummingbird, no larger than an insect.

HUMMINGBIRDS

The hummingbirds are among the most evolved and specialized birds, with truly surprising anatomical and functional characteristics. They are renowned for the magnificent colors of their plumage. In times not long past they were appreciated and exchanged like jewels. Among these birds there are some very tiny species; the *Mellisuga helenae* measures only 2.3 inches (6 centimeters) and weighs a few drams.

HOW THEY FLY

In the typical bird, the end of the wing raises the animal when it beats downwards, whereas when it returns to the starting position—or in other words is raised again—it does not generally have any lift. In hummingbirds, however, both movements lead to an upward thrust, both when the wing is lowered and when it is raised, as it is rotated at the height of the shoulder. This way of flying allows it not only to remain motionless in the air, but even to make backward movements, an achievement almost exclusive to hummingbirds. The wing beat is moreover extremely rapid, up to 75-80 times a minute, and almost silent. To perform these prodigies of flight, however, the hummingbird needs powerful pectoral muscles, the strongest, in proportion, of all living birds.

DIET

Hummingbirds are the only birds in direct competition with insects. There is no lack of other small birds that feed on flower nectar, but not exclusively; many hummingbirds are however specialized to feed only on nectar, which they suck with their long tubular tongue. All of them have a thin, pointed, and sometimes curved beak, adapted to penetrate into the corollas of flowers. Other hummingbirds, just like insects, get their heads covered with pollen when they suck the nectar and carry the pollen from one flower to another, helping in pollination and reproduction of the plant. There are however many forms that eat insects, procuring the food with darting rushes after hovering in wait for a little while.

HEAT LOSS

Hummingbirds, like all birds, are thermoregulated at 106 °F (41 °C), but their smallness leads to a big heat loss. To make up for this heat loss they must produce more energy than any other bird, and to do this they have to feed continuously. But eating from morning to evening is still not enough in many species to produce the heat necessary to keep them alive; hence the hummingbirds have recourse to another expedient: at night they turn off the conditioner thermostat and their body temperature may drop down to 64.4 °F (18 °C), thus saving a large quantity of energy. Hummingbirds are in fact the only birds that at night cease to thermoregulate themselves, just as their remote reptile ancestors did.

GREAT EATERS

Both because of the problems of thermoregulati[on] and in order to supply the energy necessary to be[at] their wings at high speed, hummingbirds need [a] considerable quantity of food, which they m[ust] devour continuously. These birds are absolute[ly] incapable of fasting; the smaller forms in particu[lar] cannot resist daytime fasting for more than 4-5 hou[rs] while the larger forms manage to reach 24 hours, af[ter] which it is death for any of them. The quantity [of] calories they absorb is extremely high; in proportio[n] man would have to eat about 300 pounds av. (1[36] kilos) of potatoes a day!

DEVELOPMENT

Naturally, hummingbird eggs are tiny, measuring on[ly] a few lines (millimeters). They are incubated for a lo[ng] time, up to 19-20 days. The technique the parents u[se] to feed the young is similar to that by which th[ey] collect nectar: they hover motionless in the air a[nd] insert the beak into the gaping mouths of the young [to] give them the food.

DISTRIBUTION

Hummingbirds are mainly concentrated in t[he] tropical forests of South America, where the heat a[nd] humidity enable them to find an abundance [of] flowers at all times; but they can move further nor[th] even into the United States, or further south, as far [as] the Tierra del Fuego in the southern tip of t[he] continent, making long migrations when the flowe[rs] blossom in these zones.

LIVERIES

The beauty of these minute birds derives not on[ly] from the color of the feathers, but also the shape th[at] some of them can take: thus in the ruby-top[az] hummingbird two long feathers adorning the tail a[re] similar to those of the lyrebird, while in others, t[he] head is adorned with splashes of color and feathers [of] unusual form. As in all birds, the brightest colors a[nd] most showy forms are flaunted by the cock birds.

THE DIVINITY BIRD

Because of its splendid colors and imposing ta[il] sometimes more than 3 feet (1 meter) long, th[e] Aztecs and Mayas venerated the quetzal (*Pharomachr[us] mocino*) as a divinity, and only the high priests a[nd] leading personalities were allowed to wear its feathe[rs] as ornament. This bird belongs to the order [of] trogoniformes and inhabits the damp mounta[in] forests of Central America. It lives on fruit a[nd] excavates a nest like the woodpecker's several fe[et] (meters) above the ground, in a rotting trunk. He[re] the hen lays two light blue eggs that are incubated [by] both parents. The survival of this species is threatene[d] by deforestation and by the pursuit of its plumes, [in] spite of the laws issued for the birds' protection.

Loddiges
spatule tail
hummingbird

Ruby-topaz
hummingbird

Frilled coquette
hummingbird

Bee
hummingbird

The ruby-throated
hummingbird lives in
the United States,
wintering in Mexico and
Central America. The
hen feeds the young
while hovering
on the wing.

male

female

Ruby-throated
hummingbird

White-
footed
racket-tail

Sword-billed
hummingbird

Sappho comet
hummingbird

White-tipped
sicklebill
hummingbird

51

Toco toucan

Left: the toco toucan is about 23 inches (60 centimeters) long, of which no less than 9 inches (23 centimeters) is taken up by the imposing beak. Used as an all-purpose tool and, despite its appearance, made of light material, it is also used by toucans to clean each other's feathers and even for lively fencing matches.

Ivory-billed woodpecker

In the United States special measures have been passed to protect the ivory-billed woodpecker's habitat, which is feared to have almost disappeared in its area of distribution covering the wild bushlands of Florida, Louisiana and South Carolina. All woodpeckers have a long tongue that can be protruded to a length of up to 4 inches (10 centimeters). Its tip is covered with hooked bristles used to extract insects from their burrows.

Woodpeckers' feet are shaped for climbing tree trunks efficiently.

26. TOUCANS, WOODPECKERS, PARROTS
(Piciformes and Psittaciformes)

TOUCANS

They belong to the order of piciformes and are unmistakable for their long, strange beak. They live in Central and South America, are tree-dwellers, and feed on fruit, insects, and even small birds. We still do not know the purpose of their long, very light beak; perhaps it evolved in earlier times for the collection of some now unknown type of food, difficult to reach otherwise; on the other hand, it could be a weapon to disconcert any aggressors by its strange shape. Toucans live in small flocks in the depths of forests, where they move in short, clumsy flights; they seem to

be joyful in character and, when they are in a group, emit raucous cries or beat their beaks noisily, sometimes throwing berries or fruit to each other; these actions may be signals linked to mating.

WOODPECKERS

Except for Australia and Madagascar, the whole world is populated with woodpeckers, very characteristic birds belonging to the order of piciformes. In order to enable them to grip onto tree-trunks vertically, woodpeckers have four toes arranged in a peculiar way: two toes in the opposite direction to the other

two. Woodpeckers have unique habits: by movi along tree-trunks and tapping them with its beak, t bird understands from the sound where there a hollows excavated by wood-eating grubs. When t woodpecker has located an insect, it drills a tunnel the trunk so that it can reach the grub. Woodpecke are also greedy eaters of ants; in one specimen mo than 900 recently caught ants were found. Their ski as wood tunnelers is also used in preparing the ne in spring the woodpecker, after finding sufficien soft wood, starts to hammer with its beak in order make a tunnel several inches (centimeters) lor which is then widened out into the nest in which t

This cockatoo raises its crest to communicate with its fellows.

Black cockatoo

Hyacinthine macaw

Scarlet macaw

One of the largest of parrots is the hyacinthine macaw, almost 40 inches (100 centimeters) in length. Macaws live among the treetops of the tropical forest. The scarlet macaw is slightly smaller.

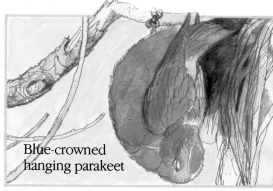

Blue-crowned hanging parakeet

The blue-crowned hanging parakeet, 6 inches (15 centimeters) long, is one of the smallest parrots.

Kakapo

The kakapo lives in the tangled mountain forests of New Zealand. It is almost incapable of flight.

gs will be laid and the young reared. The bird is
e to drill wood because of its strong, sharp beak,
d the structure of the skull and cervical vertebrae.
make the beak blow efficient, the structure of the
ne tissue of the skull is such that it can withstand
e mechanical trauma of energetic pecking.

It is debatable whether the woodpecker is a useful
harmful bird: while on the one hand it is a
racious insect-eater, on the other, by its mania for
king holes and lairs in tree-trunks, it undoubtedly
ses damage to our woodland heritage.

PARROTS

e hooked beak, colored plumes, and raucous cry
e the most obvious features distinguishing another
der of birds inhabiting tropical zones: the
ittaciformes, better known as parrots, are birds that
attract our approval as they are among the few
possessing the gift of imitating the human voice and
even modulating it, even singing snatches of songs.
Only a few species are adapted to temperate climates,
since in the tropical forests they have found an
abundance of hard fruits and nuts which they break
with their very powerful beaks. Some of them have
evolved a tongue form enabling them to suck the
nectar from flowers. Rather than fliers, parrots are
climbers and in order to move and grip branches
better they also have two claws facing forward and two
backward, which they even use to carry food to the
beak, a mode of action virtually unknown among
other birds. They are very widely distributed, from
South America to Africa, from southern Asia as far as
Australia, New Zealand, and the remote islands of the
Pacific Ocean.

Today, the only continent completely without
parrots in the wild state is Europe (in the last century
one species, the Carolina parakeet, was widespread
even in North America but was exterminated by
hunters), although fossil discoveries have
demonstrated that during the Oligocene Period (40-
50 million years ago) the French region was
populated by these birds. If they are not found as wild
fauna, they certainly are as household guests, and
their disposition for domestication has brought them
to both villages and to the palaces of the mighty.
There are reports of parrots brought to Europe in the
days of ancient Greece. Many European sovereigns, in
the increasingly frequent trading exchanges of the
Middle Ages, received them as a tribute from the
emperors of the East; this means that these
multicolored feathered friends must have been
looked upon as gifts of great price, especially if we
recall that in 1400 the pope of the time actually
appointed a "Guardian of the Parrots" to look after the
birds received as gifts.

Canadian goose

A number of Canadian geese alight in a marsh to rest and find food during migration from their nesting areas in the north of Canada, close to the Arctic Circle.

Differing from other swans in color only, the Australian black swan leads a life closely bound up with the aquatic environment. It is covered with gray down at birth and is capable of swimming and diving right from the first day of its life.

Black swan

27. MARSH BIRDS
(Anseriformes, Ciconiiformes and Gruiformes)

In the course of their evolution, some species of birds, while retaining all the characteristics of the class to which they belong, modify some features in order to colonize fresh and salt water zones. They push out into low water in order to seek food and a refuge from predatory animals, then learn to swim, or at any rate to move on and under water. Building their nests on the banks, they exploit all the resources of the surrounding vegetation, both by using it as material for construction of the nest and by adopting a camouflaged plumage that makes them practically invisible, as in the case of the bittern (ciconiiformes). In addition the bill, as in the herons (ciconiiformes), becomes long and pointed and suitable for suddenly piercing darting prey such as fish and frogs, or it may be flattened to allow sifting of the water and mud on the bottom, as in the case of the spoonbills. To be able to make progress in the water, the anseriformes and

other aquatic birds have developed webbed feet to be used as oars, while the herons and other ciconiiform members have stilt-like legs enabling them to walk in shallow water. Thus, each species of bird has selected a certain level of water, occupying it according to its physical structure and food requirements.

GEESE AND DUCKS

They belong to the order of anseriformes and are all excellent swimmers; the legs in fact end with broad webbed feet, by which the bird is propelled in the water. The long neck and flattened bill, sometimes serrated, assist in the capture of food taken directly from the water.

Although graceful and elegant when they swim, they are clumsy walkers: their legs are generally short and pushed backwards, giving them a waddling gait.

The way in which some species rise into flight is a[typical: because of the weight of its body the b must, before taking off, reach a certain speed, which obtains by "running" on the water and beating wings. After this first, and apparently clumsy pha when it is finally airborne the flight becomes stead and more elegant. Ducks and geese are in fact al fliers, capable of making extremely long journe during migrations. The flight generally ends with descent onto water that, like the take-off, is not ve elegant or assured.

Great white egret

le egret

Wading through the
shallow water with their
long legs, two marsh birds
patrol their territory.

Bittern

In its nest hidden
among the reeds a bittern
is rendered practically
invisible by its
camouflaged plumage.

Roseate
spoonbill

The roseate spoonbill lives in the swamps of
Central and South America. It feeds on molluscs,
insects and small crabs, which it catches by sifting
the water and sucking them up through
its strange, flattened bill.

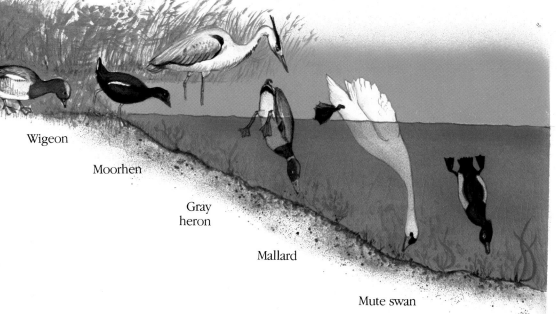

Wigeon

Moorhen

Gray
heron

Mallard

Mute swan

Tufted duck

This is how the different levels of a pond are occupied by different water
birds and their food supplies exploited. The wigeon pecks grass on the
banks. The moorhen finds food among the vegetation. The grey heron
fishes in the shallows. The mallard feeds on the surface and by half
submerging itself. The mute swan fishes by plunging its head and much
of its body beneath the water. The tufted duck
swims completely underwater.

THE BLACK SWAN

We mention this swan as representative of the vast
group. This magnificent bird (order of the
anseriformes), which nests in Australia and has been
selected as the country's emblem, lives on internal
waters or sea beaches, leading a life entirely similar to
that of the other swans. Its diet consists of water
plants and shoots, as well as small animals found in
the water or on the bottom. At one time, these animals
were widely hunted by man, especially during the
molting season. Many anseriform members in fact
lose all their wing feathers simultaneously and, until
the new ones grow, are unable to fly. During this
period, the swan is also particularly vulnerable and
can easily be caught for its meat. At one time, it was
even hunted for sport, but fortunately it is strictly
protected today. Because of its carriage and beauty the
black swan is a frequent guest of zoos.

Nightingale

The melodious song of the nightingale during courtship is especially evocative at night.

Greater bird of paradise

A Papuan warrior dressed up in bird of paradise feathers.

28. THE PASSERIFORMES

The origin of these birds is probably very ancient: a number of fossil discoveries, which are however difficult to read, would appear to date this order from the end of the era of the dinosaurs, but their development and expansion took place right through the Tertiary Era. Passeriformes by themselves account for three-fifths of all living birds, with over half a million species. Finding common characteristics among this order of birds is a difficult task since, apart from some very complex skeletal characteristics, their form and habits of life vary widely. Only the foot with toes particularly adapted to perching on branches is common to all of them: the four toes are arranged so that the well-developed big claw is opposite the other three, allowing a support to be gripped firmly.

THE NIGHTINGALE

Anyone who has heard the nightingale's song must certainly have been delighted; those who have seen it while it sang must have been equally amazed at how such a small bird could emit such sure and sparkling notes. Nightingales are spread throughout Europe and Asia, but pass the winter in Africa and thus carry out long migrations. Their main diet consists of insects they find on the ground, but they also have a liking for currants and elderberries.

THE BLACKBIRD

It is very well known in Europe as, like the sparrow, it nests in towns, parks, and gardens. It is another bird with a melodious song, but less varied than the nightingale's. It is curious to observe that blackbirds, born in the city, have no fear of humans and with a little training will even eat out of their hands, whereas blackbirds born far from urban zones are extremely shy and difficult to observe. This says a lot about the relations between humans and birds: hunters, with their ruthless selection, have forced wild animals to

Blackbirds are quite at home rummaging through the leaves of town and city gardens.

Blackbird

atin bower bird

female

male

The male satin bower bird prepares a construction of twigs, decorating it with feathers, flowers and even blue plastic objects to lure the female.

adopt behavior that would not otherwise be theirs. The blackbirds' diet is varied: insects, worms, berries, and fruit. It is always interesting in autumn or winter to see blackbirds turn over dry leaves to look for some prey underneath. These birds stand the cold very well and do not carry out big migrations; only those in the mountains come down to the plains or zones with a milder climate. Blackbirds can be domesticated and taught to whistle precise tunes.

THE SPARROW

The house sparrow is undoubtedly the most common bird in towns throughout the world. Its origin is European and Asiatic, but it has recently spread, through voluntary or involuntary importation, on the American continent and in Australia—where it has replaced local species that used the same ecological niche. Its force of expansion is based on its great resistance to the most adverse climatic conditions and its willingness to eat anything and to nest anywhere, under roofs, in bushes or trees, on broken walls, etc.

BIRDS OF PARADISE

Passeriformes do not only include birds of unassuming form and colors, but also species with extremely gaudy plumage. Birds of paradise are among these; the most renowned species, the greater bird of paradise, lives in New Guinea. The splendor and the strange forms of the plumage are in truth typical of the cock bird, as the hens are normal in form and have much more modest colors. The appellation "apoda" by which this bird is defined has a truly curious origin: the first specimens brought to Europe in the eighteenth century were embalmed without the legs, so that scholars called the species "apoda," which in Greek means "without feet."

Lyre bird

e Australian lyre bird owes its name to the long curved athers of its tail, which resemble the musical instrument.

THE LYRE BIRD

No less beautiful and fascinating is the male of the lyre bird, found only in the forests of eastern Australia. The size of the body is similar to that of a pheasant, but with a very long tail that may reach almost 5 feet (1.5 meters). Unfortunately, it is rare to see these birds as they are very shy, and at the slightest suspect noise flee to hide in the depths of the bush; this is perhaps what has saved them from extermination, as they are much sought after by zoos and embalmers.

CROWS

They are robust birds of the order of passeriformes, with a strong beak capable of tearing fragments of meat from a carcass; they can eat anything, and at times attack like birds of prey. They are also perhaps the most intelligent birds, still within the limits of what was said in Chap. 16. The raven, found in Europe, North America, Asia, and North Africa is the most typical representative of the family and one of the largest, with a wingspan of nearly 5 feet (1.5 meters). Ravens are easily domesticated and can learn words, sounds, or the cries of other animals.

Raven

The raven can measure up to 23 inches (60 centimeters) in length. It is very strong and does not fear even large birds of prey.

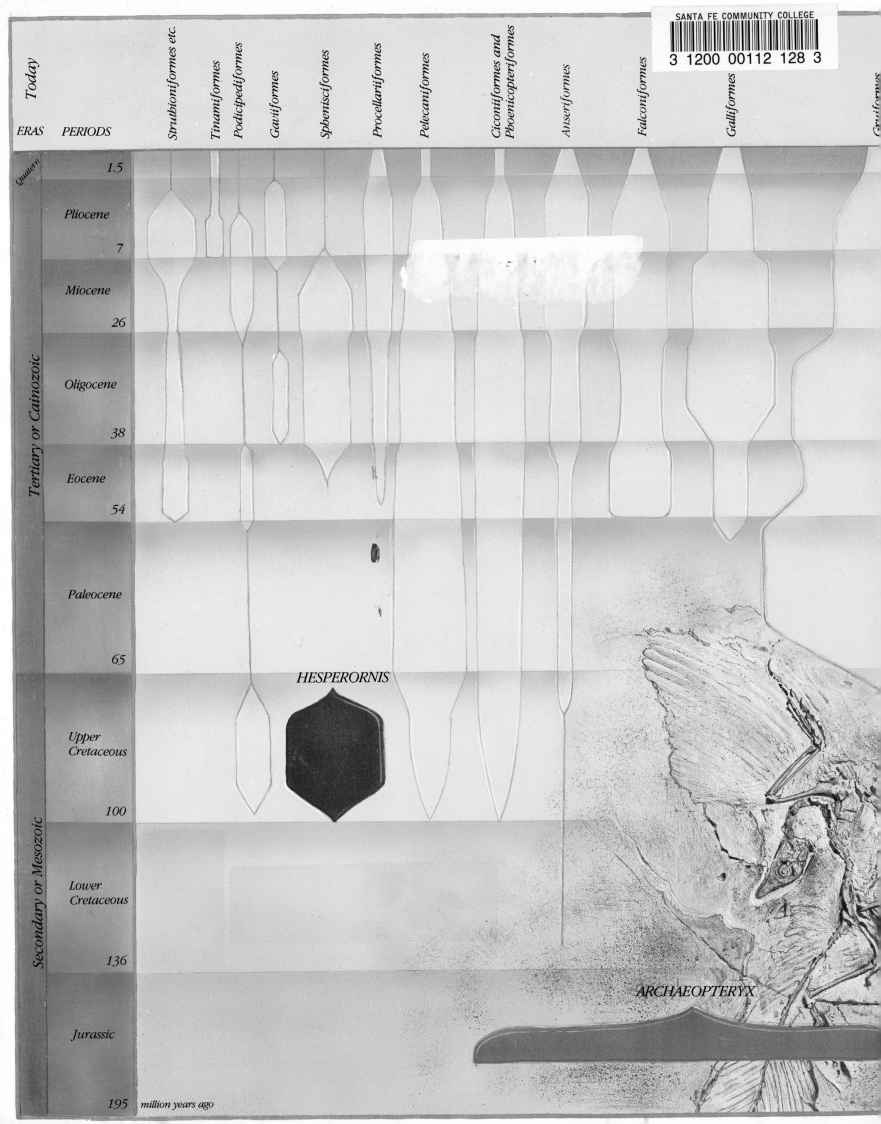

Today

ERAS   PERIODS

Struthioniformes etc.

Tinamiformes

Podicipediformes

Gaviiformes

Sphenisciformes

Procellariiformes

Pelecaniformes

Ciconiiformes and Phoenicopteriformes

Anseriformes

Falconiformes

Galliformes

Gruiformes

Quatern.   1.5

Pliocene

7

Miocene

26

Oligocene

38

Eocene

54

Paleocene

65

Tertiary or Cainozoic

Upper
Cretaceous

100

HESPERORNIS

Lower
Cretaceous

136

Secondary or Mesozoic

Jurassic

ARCHAEOPTERYX

195   *million years ago*